STRUCTURE OF THE EGO

STRUCTURE OF THE EGO

An Anatomic and Physiologic Interpretation
of the Psyche
Based on the Psychology of Otto Rank

By

LOVELL LANGSTROTH, M.D.

STANFORD UNIVERSITY PRESS
STANFORD, CALIFORNIA

LONDON: GEOFFREY CUMBERLEGE
OXFORD UNIVERSITY PRESS

1955

STANFORD UNIVERSITY PRESS
STANFORD, CALIFORNIA

PUBLISHED IN GREAT BRITAIN AND INDIA
BY GEOFFREY CUMBERLEGE,
OXFORD UNIVERSITY PRESS,
LONDON AND BOMBAY

HENRY M. SNYDER & COMPANY, INC.
440 FOURTH AVENUE, NEW YORK 16

W. S. HALL & COMPANY
510 MADISON AVENUE, NEW YORK 22

PRINTED AND BOUND IN THE UNITED STATES
OF AMERICA BY STANFORD UNIVERSITY PRESS

Library of Congress Catalog Card Number: 55–9583

To the Memory of
DORA WINN LANGSTROTH

CONTENTS

FIGURES

PROLOGUE

Psychology, in the sense used here, is based on observation, study, and interpretation of man's behavior. But the most important of these is interpretation, and since any interpretation is a subjective process its correctness depends on the maturity, experience, and perspicuity of the observer. Thus even though one observer has a considerable fund of psychological knowledge the peculiarities of behavior in a subject may entirely escape him and still be quite evident to a second observer who has what has been called an intuitive sense but would better be called perception or insight in regard to behavior of others. There is no magic about intuition. It derives from a similarity of structure and a self-awareness that makes its possessor conscious of processes going on in a subject which the first observer has not experienced himself. This makes for great differences of opinion in this field and is the reason why the acceptance of this kind of knowledge has been so stubbornly resisted. One type of mind will not accept any psychology as factual unless it can be measured, while another much prefers to rely on knowledge gained intuitively rather than on measurements. The first may develop a test which purports to measure and does measure the ability of an individual to perform certain mental calisthenics or to remember certain facts; the second is more interested in the processes by which these calisthenics are performed, for to him these processes bring him nearer to an understanding of psychic function.

Dr. Otto Rank had this intuitive sense very strongly developed. To those unfamiliar with his name it should be stated that he was a doctor of philosophy, not a physician, that he was a brilliant scholar, a prolific writer, and a successful psychotherapist. His natural endowment and his philosophical training must have given him a great adaptability for psychological understanding because he worked with Sigmund Freud in the treatment of patients for over twenty years, though, like Freud, he was never "psychoanalyzed." This clinical work formed the basis for independent views which were published from time to time but, for the most part, were unacceptable to the main psychoanalytical group and thus led to Rank's definitive separation from Freudianism.

Rank's association with Freud began at an early age and it was at Freud's suggestion that he directed his university studies toward the cultural and nonmedical aspects of the psychoanalytic movement.[1] This symbiotic association was undoubtedly valuable to both men: Freud's medical training tended in a general way to give form and definition to such of his concepts

[1] See Fay B. Karpf, "Art and Artist [a biographical sketch]," Ch. I, *The Psychology and Psychotherapy of Otto Rank* (New York: Philosophical Library, 1953).

1

as the id, the ego, and the superego, while Rank's cultural background tended to broaden and humanize them and to extend them into philosophical and even religious fields. After their separation, and apparently as a reaction to it, Rank's writing shows more and more a loss of definition and form. Thus Freud's influence is still very apparent in Rank's *Grundzüge einer Genetischen Psychologie—Auf Grund der Psychoanalyse der Ichstruktur* (Leipzig und Wien: Franz Deuticke, 1927) but somewhat less so in *Gestaltung und Ausdruck der Persönlichkeit* (Deuticke, 1928), while in *Wahrheit und Wirklichkeit—Entwurf einer Philosophie des Seelischen* (Deuticke, 1929) it seems almost completely absent. This last book with its introduction of the will psychology marks Rank's complete break from Freud, but one familiar with the genetic psychology will easily see that the same general principles are maintained, though clothed in quite different garb.[2] From that point on Rank continued to call his work "will psychology"[3] and his expression became more and more abstruse until at times it is very difficult to know just what he means to say. Through all this later work, however, it is crystal clear that his emphasis was on the dynamics of the psychotherapeutic situation and that this emphasis was a most important one in therapy.[4]

For some years the present writer has applied Rank's principles of psychotherapy to neurotic patients, with a growing conviction of their clinical effectiveness. This conviction gradually culminated in the belief that the forces he described must originate in actual nuclei and reach each other by way of actual tracts in the central nervous system. Rank's ego structure was not apparent on superficial study but its form evolved gradually as the present writer found it possible to identify these forces and to follow their development in himself as well as in his patients. When at last given diagrammatic form, it was found to duplicate closely the structure and some of the connections given the diencephalon by modern anatomists and physiologists.

The present work is based mainly on a study of the first three books that Rank wrote after his separation from Freud; it deals predominantly with

---

[2] See "Erkennen und Erleben," p. 28, in *Wahrheit und Wirklichkeit*, translated into English by Jessie Taft as *Truth and Reality* and published by Alfred A. Knopf, Inc., 1936; and compare with the diagram of the ego structure shown later.

[3] See Otto Rank, *Will Therapy* (New York: Alfred A. Knopf, Inc., 1936).

[4] The present writer made it possible for Rank to visit the San Francisco Bay region in 1936 and thus had a brief personal contact with him. During that visit he gave four talks, one of them arranged through the courtesy of the late Dr. Ray Lyman Wilbur at Stanford University. This was an opportunity for Rank to present his views to a selected group and his way of preparing for it indicates his casual attitude toward the important matter of form in self-expression: he dictated what he was to say to a stenographer at the Medical School in the morning and read her transcription the same afternoon to the University audience. Such casualness seems to the present writer to explain completely the admitted difficulty in extracting Rank's thought from his way of expressing it, for it is axiomatic that simple clear expression is achieved only by the exercise of infinite patience, great care, and frequent revision.

structure and for this reason Freud's influence on these three books has been indicated above. The first, called *Fundamentals of Genetic Psychology on the Basis of Psychoanalysis of the Ego Structure*, was delivered in lecture form at the New York School of Social Work in 1926 and published in German in 1927 (Deuticke). The second, a later part of his genetic psychology, he called *Development and Expression of Personality*. It was published in German in 1928 (Deuticke). The third volume, *Truth and Reality*, was published in German in 1929, in English in 1936. The material in these books has been freely used and rearranged in such sequence and form as to make it more suitable for illustration by diagram and so, perhaps, to make its meaning clearer than in the original.

The resulting diagram represents the ego structure and, as will be shown in Chapter III, finds an almost exact counterpart in the central nervous system, whose anatomy has been so laboriously and painstakingly worked out by modern scientists. Knowledge of this anatomic counterpart was gained from study of the diencephalon and its connections with the cortex. The texts used were John Farquhar Fulton, *Physiology of the Nervous System*, New York: Oxford University Press, 1949; Stephen Walter Ranson, *The Anatomy of the Nervous System* (revised by Sam Lillard Clark), Philadelphia and London: W. B. Saunders Company, 1947; and J. F. Fulton, editor, *A Textbook of Physiology* (by William H. Howell), Philadelphia and London: W. B. Saunders Company, 1949. While a great effort has been made to present the connections accurately, some small liberties have been taken when their course was not definitely known and when the clinical facts seemed to warrant it. For the view has been taken that such a course might contribute to further development and understanding of the anatomic structure.

The development of the ego structure and the discovery of its anatomic counterpart have made it possible to synthesize them into a workable understanding of brain structure and to formulate a hypothesis for its function. Many who think highly of Rank's later books may feel that the present work based on his earlier ones smacks too much of Freud. But the present writer feels that the anatomic counterpart bears out his contention that the earlier and later books merely supplement each other, that the former relate to detailed structure and the latter to broader, more general principles.

The process by which an understanding of Rank's work has been gained is based on the experience of applying it practically and can best be described as digestion and assimilation. It is inevitable therefore that the present work should differ in some minor respects from his rather vaguely stated views, first because a sycophantic following of them would be degrading, second because in this field no two different individuals can view the same material in exactly the same way, and third because of discovery of a possible anatomic basis for the ego. Rank himself would be the first to make allowance for these differences.

It seems important to point out also that the moral relativism presently under discussion in our universities is a problem with which this book is directly concerned. For the anatomic counterpart of the ego structure gives man's conscience a possible structural basis and indicates that undue freeing of the sexual impulse often eventuates in destruction of both the individual and his environment. Moral values will be shown later to be practical matters of survival, even of life or death, to the neurotic patient, who may usually be brought through treatment to the point where he can see that he has some choice in the matter. But his negativism is so strong that they can never be imposed on him and the degree to which his self-development will continue thereafter must vary with each and every individual.

Thanks are due to Dr. Victor E. Hall and to Dr. Robert S. Turner of Stanford University for helpful criticism of the earliest beginnings of this book and to Dr. J. M. Crismon and Dr. Ronald Grant, also of Stanford University, for perusal of and comment on a later draft. And the author is indebted to his son, Dr. Lovell Langstroth, Jr., whose advice contributed greatly to the form in which the work is presented.

I

PARTS OF THE SELF AND THEIR DISCOVERY

Psychological Principles Derived from the Psychotherapeutic Situation[1]

Man's dualism.—The idea has long been current that man has two natures, one physical, the other spiritual, and that each struggles to dominate the other. Good and evil, sin and guilt, and in recent times, individualism and collectivism, or positivism and negativism are all variations on the same main theme. This dualism is written into all the great religions. It is these that have been man's guide toward integration of the physical and the spiritual, and have recorded at the same time his upward development. For throughout history the mark of the superior man has been the control and use of the physical by the spiritual, the struggle toward an ideal ("spiritual" is here used to translate the German *seelisch*).

In earlier times, then, the responsibility for this dualism was easily attributed to supernatural beings. But growing self-awareness and self-realization, together with a lessening belief in the supernatural, have forced him to seek and find the good and evil and their resolution in himself. The progress of *this* development is written in the psychologies. It is now in these that he seeks for salvation. But his ideal is still the same, integration of the physical and spiritual.

In modern times the struggle of the physical nature to dominate the spiritual takes a new form. Crime and corruption in government may be symptomatic of this struggle in the man of action, psychoneurosis or psychosis in the man of thought. For the symptomatology of these diseases always masks a bad will and a bad conscience. Rationalize instinct, or—in natural science terms—libido, if you will, but in the last analysis guilt always ensues as a last unavoidable, inescapable fact.

The biological self.—In the sense used here this is that part of the ego that acts for its own purposes, in pursuit of satisfactions, and is the psychological counterpart, the executive of the physical self. Fixed as to quantity and quality, but susceptible of development within its given limits, it must

[1] Most of the material given here may be found in "Charakter und Selbst," *Gestaltung und Ausdruck der Persönlichkeit*, p. 21.

adjust in some way or other to its environment, and the expression of this adjustment is behavior.

The social self.—This is that part of the ego which before Rank's work was considered to be adopted from the environment. But his conception of the social self as a force present at birth and capable of modification by the milieu through identification gives it an independent existence. It is to this modified social self that the biological self must adjust, and thus *indirectly* to the environment.

The character.—This begins to form almost from the moment of birth and results from the adjustment between the biological self and the social self as modified by the environment. Three elements thus participate in its formation: social self, environment, and biological self. Adult character is a summation of the experiences of this adjustment; it governs behavior and normally makes it acceptable to the milieu.

The average man.—It is evident that in the average man the social and biological selves are more or less in harmony. His social self and ideals are formed under the influence of the incoming stream of sensory impressions from the environment and are accepted by the biological self, which adjusts to them without much conflict; the individual and his environment are at peace with each other.

The creative personality.—In the creative personality either the biological or the social self is stronger than the other. When the biological self is stronger the individual's behavior may begin to differ so much from what we have come to expect of his previous character and environment as to surprise us and even him; his biological self escapes the restraint imposed by his character and appears as quite different from his social self; the two are not in harmony as in the average man. In this case the individual is impulsive and his impulse tends to result in action which is creative to the extent that it overcomes the social self: positively creative when the ideal toward which it strives is ethical, negatively creative when the ideal is antisocial; if he has conflict between the two selves it appears after the action has occurred, and the influence of the social self then appears as remorse. But when the social self is stronger than the biological self it is not so much the behavior which begins to differ from what we have come to expect of the character, as the thought. For this type is restrained and his impulse turns inward in thought instead of outward in action; he, too, may be creative, but in the field of thought: positively creative when the ideal is toward social betterment, negatively creative when this ideal does not exist and the social self turns in against the biological self in neurotic self-criticism. When there is conflict between the two selves in this case, it occurs within and prevents action.

In the types described above in whom either the biological self or the social self predominates, the adjustment of one to the other is made with great struggle. It is this struggle which characterizes the creative person on the one hand and the neurotic on the other. The first, the creative person, finds it possible to externalize the conflict and so solve it, the man of action by a series of actions and failures through which he learns to overcome the external difficulties, the man of thought by a pictorial or verbal representation of it in art, literature, philosophy, etc. The second, the neurotic, either keeps the conflict within himself and so gradually destroys himself, or externalizes it by projecting it onto a sexual partner. And since one neurotic usually marries another and each soon projects the self with which he is in conflict onto the other, the process is continued indefinitely without resolution.

The spiritual self.—It now becomes apparent that the spiritual self, mentioned above as opposed to the physical self, is neither the social self nor the biological self. It is rather an ethical part of the personality whose demands are above and beyond those of the environment. Adjustment to this spiritual self by the biological self means a struggle to modify the demands of the biological self until they can bear the scrutiny of this ethical self without guilt feeling.

This general consideration of the man of action and the man of thought gives us a beginning insight into their structure; it enables us to place the neurotic in the second category, and to see that his social self is turned in against his biological self and thus impedes his development. Knowledge of this development, and thus of the psyche in the sense used here, really began with Freud's discovery of the psychotherapeutic situation (Rank declares that Freud discovered this situation but interpretated it as a "transference" from the Oedipus situation).

The Psychotherapeutic Situation[2]

As used by the present writer the psychotherapeutic situation involves a neurotic person and the psychotherapist. The neurotic is "object hungry" because he has been unable to establish a satisfactory object relationship (love relationship), and so, under the conditions of physical passivity implied by this situation, is usually ready to put aside the restraints imposed by his character, and to project his real biological self onto the therapist. For perhaps the first time in his life he finds a person who accepts him as he really is, listens to everything he has to say, and, while interpreting much of this in psychological terms, does not criticize or advise. That is to say, the role of the therapist is purely interpretive; he does not project his own self (his ideas and ideals) onto the patient; he is not an active participant. Under

[2] See Translator's Introduction, "The Discovery of the Analytic Situation," in *Will Therapy* (New York: Alfred A. Knopf, Inc., 1936).

these conditions the neurotic's projections are at first entirely negative, i.e., consist of complaints first about himself, and then of others, but gradually take on a positive character which often enough finally culminates in more or less veiled expressions of attachment to the therapist. At this point he feels quite sure of himself and shows in various ways that he desires to finish with the therapist and depart. Then the therapist sets a date for termination of the treatments. This precipitates a crisis in the relationship; the patient loses his self-confidence and usually is in great distress. The reason for this change is that setting the final date makes him realize that his self-confidence depends on the psychotherapeutic relationship and was a denial of his infantile attachment to the therapist. The conflict during this period is between his desire to get well and leave and the feeling which makes him cling to the therapist like a child. When this is pointed out to him the conflict is resolved as he gradually overcomes his feeling attachment to the therapist by accepting the responsibility for his suffering instead of projecting it onto the therapist and thus hating him. During all his struggle the patient learns to dissociate thought and feeling from action and thus is able to undergo the necessary psychological changes without the danger of compromising himself by expressing the intermediary stages in action. The psychotherapeutic situation is thus an artificially induced but one-sided feeling experience which, because one side of it is controlled by the therapist, permits the patient to pass through a phase of development previously missed. It is the most constructive element in psychotherapy.

But there is an additional element in this situation, namely a revelation of material that has hitherto been unconscious and a backward projection of this by the therapist onto the patient's historical past so as to tie it up with the patient's early development; this projection acts intellectually as an explanation of past difficulties and a guide to future development. The fact that one is still attached to one's mother and afraid of one's father (castration complex) is an example of this knowledge.

These revelations are deduced from dreams by interpretation and it is largely from this kind of material that a genetic psychology has been constructed. Certain elements occur regularly in almost every case, and since the therapist is careful never to project his own ideas onto the patient or to make suggestions, it may be assumed that they appear spontaneously and are reproductions not so much of earlier events as of infantile tendencies which remain in the personality. The patient is better off to get no knowledge not directly connected with his own reactions in the psychotherapeutic situation. In this case it may benefit him by increasing his self-perception; without the accompanying reaction it may do more harm than good.

But some patients do not produce this kind of material and the therapist comes to realize that sometimes he must deal more with the general reactions which occur in the psychotherapeutic situation, i.e., with the patient's positive and negative reactions, than with the facts of genetic psychology. The results may be equally good in both cases. These positive and negative reactions, or tendencies, are abstractions which reduce the more detailed facts on which genetic psychology is founded to more general principles which will become clearer with discussion of the will psychology. They are there represented as emanating from two sources, the will and opposing will, which have made possible this physiologic and anatomic interpretation of the psyche.

Freud saw the patient's negative expressions as resistance, and went to great lengths to break down this resistance through psychotherapy. To him it was most important that the patient see the cause of this resistance intellectually by accepting the therapist's interpretation of it. This began a battle of wills and made the therapy a long drawn out affair. The positive and negative expressions Freud called a transference, and saw them as a repetition of the adolescent period, when the mother was the object on which the developing sexuality of youth was projected, and the father the external object whose restraint it was necessary to accept. He found a parallel between this and the well-known Oedipus myth, in which the hero kills off his father, marries his mother, and then perishes because of his guilt. Freud's interpretation made the struggle between the self and the environment a purely biological and materialistic one; the guilt arose from the father-son relationship and was overcome by identification with him and the establishment of a superego. It was related to an outer object and thus given a purely moral value, whose force was emphasized by the threat of castration on the one hand, or the reward of the privileges of a father on the other, like the punishment and reward in the morality of the Old Testament. But this mythological interpretation was not only a purely moral one; it emphasized the struggle between the biological compulsion of sexuality and the force of the outer moral authority in such a way as to leave the ego almost helpless between them.

Rank saw the patient's negative expressions as emanating from a social self which was stronger than average and therefore offered more opposition to the biological self, but which had to be accepted by both the neurotic and the therapist before the patient could come to terms with it. If the therapist attacks this force he is really trying to do away with it by assuming the role of a moral authority, and this merely prolongs the struggle the patient has always had with his environment. But if he waits and listens he soon finds that the patient shows a guilt reaction toward these negativisms and thus proves that he has within himself an authority which is ethical in its judgments, not only of the negative expressions but also of the positive expressions already mentioned above in connection with the psychotherapeutic situation. Rank's whole method of treatment is an attempt to bring out this ethical judgment of the patient, which soon transforms the negative expressions of hatred into positive expressions of "love."

In this conception, then, the social self is not merely adopted from the outer world, as in Freud's view, but exists in the individual at birth as a negative force which in one type of the creative person and in the neurotic is stronger than average and thus often opposes not only outer reality but also the biological self. This opposing force is overcome by the biological self in the creative person but overcomes the biological self in the neurotic and impedes his development.

II

THE PSYCHIC MECHANISMS[1]

The psychotherapeutic situation not only permits the patient to put aside his character and project onto the therapist his biological self in its immature form, but it also gives the therapist an opportunity to observe and study the mechanisms which have operated to prolong the immaturity and which are used during the period of development and recovery.

Projection.—The first of these mechanisms, projection, has already been mentioned as the process by which the individual reveals his biological self to the therapist. The first negative projections in the psychotherapeutic situation are complaints about the self and other persons. But the therapist soon finds that the complaints about others are often not justified, that, to use a common example, the hatred of the son for the father does not always derive from cruelty on the part of the father but instead from opposition of the son to the father, which is justified by making the father out as cruel. This negative projection is thus a method of attributing to another person a force which really arises in the self and is revealed to the therapist as primarily sadistic. When the projections become positive in character the whole attitude of the patient toward the therapist and toward outer reality changes as his gratitude, feeling, and/or libido find expression in various more or less disguised ways. It becomes evident that the patient is projecting these onto the therapist and sees him as their source, that the negative projections have for the time disappeared under the influence of these positive ones.

Identification.—It seems obvious that one could not and would not practice psychotherapy unless he believed that the patient could get well and unless he believed in himself. This is certainly a *positive* attitude in him and is revealed in his general attitude but is not necessarily stated in words. It is this positive attitude with which the patient identifies. The therapist certainly does not "love" the patient (as the mother loves her child) and the patient does not necessarily "love" the therapist because he identifies with him on this positive level. The "love" the patient may manifest is merely evidence of the thankfulness and gratitude he bears him. This is usually symbolized in sexual terms because the human being expresses himself in this way.

[1] See "Die Psychischen Mechanismen und ihre Auswirkungen," in *Grundzüge einer Genetischen Psychologie,* I Teil, III (Leipzig and Wien: Franz Deuticke, 1927).

11

Identification is thus a taking into the ego structure of something from the environment, in this case the therapist's positive attitude. This is a *positive* identification. It is beneficial and unavoidable but we must indicate here that what the therapist tells the patient at this particular time in the psychotherapeutic situation may also be taken in, though it will not necessarily be useful to him and may even be harmful. The idea is to give him as little as possible ideology with which to identify so as to force him to be creative enough to develop his own. For the stronger his bonds of identification with the therapist become, the more difficult he will find it to break away from him and get well. But with the absence of any positive projections from the therapist the patient soon shows a growing desire to get away and feels guilty about this because of his positive identification with him. At this time a definite date is set for conclusion of the treatments.

Denial, or "Verleugnung."—The result of setting this date is usually that the patient shows evidence of conflict and that, along with withdrawal of the positive projections, the negative projections reappear, the patient often declaring that all his symptoms have returned. This is as much as to say that the therapist has failed in his treatment and thus constitutes a negative projection onto him. At this moment the patient's fate hangs in the balance. If the therapist reassures him the patient may be lost, because this only makes him dependent on the therapist again and prevents his getting away. He has to be shown that his suffering and complaints are attempts to win this reassurance from the therapist as a sign of affection and are a direct contradiction of his previously expressed desire to get away, and that the only reassurance that will do him any good is his own. He must be forced to resolve his immature attachment to the therapist on the one hand and his desire to get away from him on the other, and he can do this only by overcoming his attachment; to go away hating him would jeopardize his recovery. Gradually his suffering then diminishes and by the end of the therapy it has generally disappeared. This change has been described in some detail because it illustrates the mechanism of *"Verleugnung,"* or denial. Denial is normally used to cushion the shock of change at various periods of development when one stage must be abandoned and a new attitude taken toward the future but is given up when the readjustment can be made. The therapist sees it operating in this way toward the end of the psychotherapy. When the date has been set for termination of the treatments the patient denies his desire to leave the therapist by protesting that he is still ill and in need of more help. This is a denial of the future reality and a clinging to his neurotic past in terms of the patient-therapist or child-mother relationship. The fact that he now has to face this problem shows that he has failed to overcome it in the past and that this is what has kept him immature. If he fails to overcome it now, then the negative projections onto the therapist continue and he may leave hating him and thus fail to get well. By contrast with those who do overcome it and do get well, he must be considered as leaving the therapist, just as he had previously left the mother, in a condition of negative identification; in both cases it was because he could not overcome the denial.

But sometimes it is not feeling for the object that is denied but moral responsibility for actions, and then the denial may obtrude during the early part of the psychotherapeutic situation as a major cause of difficulty. This is because it is an attempt to break down the sequence of cause and effect. The patient has acted in such a way as to bring about disagreeable reactions on the part of others or disagreeable reactions on the part of his own soma but at the same time has denied responsibility for it. If he continues to do this he cannot get well. In such a case one must await the appearance of *evidence* of his own knowledge of this responsibility so as to allow him to accuse himself, so to speak, the therapist merely acting as a mirror which reflects the true situation to him. Otherwise the therapist will take the position of a moral arbiter, oppose his interpretation or his will to that of the patient and thus initiate a contest that drags on interminably. However, the purpose of this book is to point out the parallel which seems to exist between the ego structure and the diencephalon; it is not a manual of treatment and such details as the above must therefore be omitted.

Negative identification.—Negative identification is, of course, the reverse of positive identification and means a harboring of resentment toward the object because of real or fancied injuries or because of withdrawal of favors. If the resentment is suppressed through fear of the object then this establishes the object as a punishing authority onto whom the responsibility for the resulting suffering is projected. The patient should therefore be helped to express his feeling of resentment toward the therapist at this time because this helps overcome his denial.

Positive identification acts as a means of establishing the object as an ideal which grants favors, and negative identification as a means of establishing the object as an authority which deals out punishment. Both depend primarily on projection. The denial mechanism operates between the two at various levels of biological development; through it the individual clings to the earlier level by denying the reality of the necessary change.

III

THE DEVELOPMENTAL STAGES[1]

From the immaturity of the neurotic and the projection of his biological self (biological level) onto the therapist in the psychotherapeutic situation it has been possible to segregate neurotics into groups and to see that their difficulties stem from a misuse of the denial mechanism at a time when one developmental stage must be given up and another begun; the denial is continued instead of overcome. The evidence shows that these stages are separated by (1) the weaning time, (2) the period of toilet training to cleanliness, (3) the advent of a sibling, (4) the discovery of sex differences.

1. The weaning time separates the oral from the narcissistic stage. At weaning an infant may refuse all nourishment for several days, evidently because of the shock of change. By analogy with the reactions of the patient to the shock of setting the final date one may reconstruct the sequence of reactions he must have had at this earlier time: the libido previously satisfied at the breast is denied this outlet; it is transferred to the hand (thumbsucking) and then to the genitalia (infantile masturbation is an observable fact), where a substitute satisfaction is thus at hand. This explanation of the development of narcissism is thus a logical one for events observed at this period. The nipple (as a symbol for the mother) is denied together with all signs of affection (positive projections are withdrawn), and irritation is shown (negative projections) toward the mother. It is usual for this denial to be partially overcome and for a feeling relationship of a different type to be established with the mother. But since the homosexual is unable to project his libido onto a woman at maturity one must suppose that this is because he has not overcome the denial of the mother, just as in the psychotherapeutic situation an occasional neurotic will continue his denial of the therapist after the final date is set and go away hating him, i.e., refusing to get well.

2. At the time of toilet training to cleanliness the child must learn to evacuate his bladder and rectum at specific places and times, and not where and when he pleases. Observation of children shows that they have no natural feeling of repugnance to feces and may even like to get their hands in it; the idea that it is nasty or dirty is acquired by identification with the mother. During this period of training the child must therefore renounce one stage and accept another. The character of the mother has great in-

[1] See "Zur Genese der Genitalitat," in *Grundzüge einer Genetischen Psychologie*, I Teil (Leipzig and Wien: Franz Deuticke, 1927), p. 69.

fluence at this time. If she is strict and stern in regard to dirtiness and even threatens punishment for disregard of it, her attitude is in marked contrast with the natural inclination of the child to be indifferent to it. Evidence collected from dreams during psychotherapy shows that the child reacts to this by denial of the mother (her perineal region), i.e., hates the mother but suppresses this thought through fear and so identifies with her at the same time. This is a negative identification. The child may well project the idea of dirtiness onto the mother and think that because she lays so much emphasis on it she herself must be dirty, a thought sometimes supported by the odor of menstruation, etc. If this denial is continued the so-called rectal character may be formed in the child. The principal traits of these persons are order, neatness, and cleanliness carried to an extreme and are most often found in females; this coprophobia may result in obstinate constipation. Since the vagina is close to the anal opening and the urethral orifice adjacent to it, the whole perineal area may come under the same ban of dirtiness, and sexual guilt feeling ensue. In the neurotic woman this may cause frigidity— the social self overcomes the biological self—but in the pervert the reaction is just the opposite: the biological self overcomes the social self as represented by the mother, and pleasure is found in connection with the anus and feces, in coprophilia, and in *defiance* of the mother. But even without this extreme outcome found in frigidity on the one hand or perversion on the other the imposition by the mother of the social restraints on freedom of expression in regard to urination, masturbation, or defecation has this result: the child projects the restraint onto the mother where it remains and acts as a superego during the narcissistic period; violation of these social restraints then causes guilt.

3. With the advent of a younger sibling the child often loses much of the mother's attention and demonstration of affection and reacts to this loss by denying the newcomer. This often means a wish to do away with the new arrival: let the stork take it away again. The denial thus involves not only negative projection onto the new sibling, but, because of the desire to take its place, imitative behavior, and thus negative identification with it. The child may thus take on enough of the sibling's traits to form a split in its personality, that is, to give it two superegos and two different developmental ideals.

4. With recognition of sex differences and the beginning of sex maturation the narcissistic stage comes gradually to an end. The libido which was first gratified at the breast and then displaced downward is again projected outward and, as the dream discloses, frequently onto the first object, the mother. This is the period of the Oedipus situation. The neurotic male uses the denial mechanism again here and this time applies it to the female genitalia (as a symbol of the mother). He avoids mention and consideration

of these parts and seems to have what might be called a blind spot for them. This denial makes him fearful of women (as he has hated and feared the mother) and afraid that he cannot play a man's part (castration complex) and keeps him halfway in the narcissistic stage which the normal overcome promptly.

One sees that the thing denied at the time of change between the various stages is the part of the woman most important for that particular stage (the nipple, the anus and urethral orifice, the vagina) and is used symbolically to represent the mother. This led Rank to his conception that in the psychotherapeutic situation the immature neurotic used the therapist as a symbol for the mother and that the reactions manifested in that situation undoubtedly were the same as those which occurred in actual development. Other evidence to support this conception will be developed later on, in Chapter VIII.

IV

GENETIC PSYCHOLOGY[1]

The present writer has gone into some detail in describing the developmental stages and the psychic mechanisms disclosed by psychotherapy so as to prepare the ground for an understanding of genetic psychology. In constructing what seemed to him the probable developmental pattern from birth to maturity Rank used a vast amount of material gathered from the work of other therapists as well as his own.[2] Since this pattern forms an important part of the ego structure it will be briefly outlined here.

The embryo in the various stages of its intra-uterine existence reproduces earlier more primitive forms of life, and the ego is here conceived to follow a somewhat similar developmental course after birth. This concept has already been suggested by the reactions occurring during psychotherapy. Both of the ego's two original primitive elements are modified by the maternal environment so as to give them human characteristics. Its first cry and spasmodic movements, which occur with the onset of consciousness of outer stimuli, would thus be interpreted as signs of irritation, a protest, as it were, against being so roughly torn from a paradisaical stage of union with the mother and thrust rudely into this world; they are negative like the first projections of the neurotic in the psychotherapeutic situation. The infant's first nursing is apparently a mere satisfaction of hunger and libido, and as such shows no characteristic difference from that of any other animal. In this sense the first nursing is positive, but primitive; its later counterpart might be the libido of the criminal rapist. It does not find a parallel in the psychotherapeutic situation because in the neurotic the social self is turned in against the ego structure and thus restrains the originally primitive libido.

Normal Development

Primitive dualism.—The same dualism manifested in the psychotherapeutic situation is thus carried back to the postnatal period when, except for autonomic activities, the mouth is the only medium of emotional expression and the only organ to show co-ordinated conscious activity. It seems appropriate therefore that Rank should represent this dualism by forces which he called oral sadismus and oral libido. Oral libido is a positive ego expression

[1] See *Grundzüge einer Genetischen Psychologie,* I Teil (Genetischen Teil), p. 67.
[2] Credit is given to them in Rank's original work and therefore is omitted here.

of infantile sexuality, and oral sadismus a negative ego expression; but both are primitive. The present writer assumes these forces to emanate from nuclei in the ego structure. The first would be the origin of the positive impulses manifested during the psychotherapeutic situation, the second the origin of the negative expressions.

Positive identification.—But the primitive picture shown at birth gradually changes. In response to the mother's love the infant identifies positively with her and the signs of irritation diminish. This change is a counterpart of what is seen in the psychotherapeutic situation where the negative projections diminish as the positive ones make their appearance; this is the pattern Rank has evidently projected back to the infantile situation in his "genetic psychology." The negative projections dam back, so to speak, into the ego structure to act as restraint which modifies the primitive oral libido at its source; for the positive projections shown by the infant's smiling response to the mother's love are a modification of the original primitive oral libido.

Common examples of positive identification.—This damming back of the negative projections which play such a prominent and effective part in psychotherapy will perhaps be better understood if illustrated by phenomena which are commonly observed in everyday life. Take for example the "conversion of a sinner" at a religious revival meeting, for "sinning" is merely an expression of negativism against the outer world. This conversion means that under the influence of a stronger and more dynamic personality a man has suddenly been "reborn," that is to say, become more positive. With this his negativism disappears. But where does it go? Such a strong force cannot evaporate into nothing. Or take, for another example, what the love of a good woman may do for a man. He may give up most of his minor vices and thereafter devote himself to her and his family. Under the influence of this positive, outgoing stream the negative expressions disappear for the most part. One may ask again what becomes of them?

Reciprocal relation between positive and negative.—In the two examples given above the positive side appears as the negative side disappears. There is then a reciprocal relation between positivism and negativism which is brought about by an outside factor. Under this influence the negative dams back to make the positive less primitive. The change occurs gradually over a considerable period of time in the adult but quickly in the infant when outside conditions are good. This modification of the primitive positivism occurs through the ego structure and must be elucidated at this point.

Mechanism of modification of primitive oral libido.—The ego structure was first conceived as a chain of four nuclei joined together like a closed ring of carbon atoms as follows:

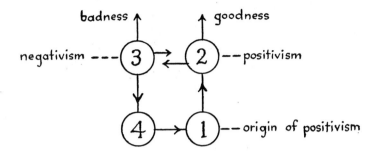

The negative force emanating from *3* dams back spontaneously under the influence of the mother's love, i.e., the force called oral sadismus, instead of passing upward and outward as badness, is exerted downward through *4* to restrain *1*, which is the origin of the primitive oral libido. This is the mechanism by which the primitive oral libido is modified by positive identification.

Negative identification: denial of the nipple.—As positive identification with the mother becomes established the infant may become irritated when she withdraws the breast and react negatively; the hunger is satisfied but the libido is not. The withdrawal arouses oral sadismus which is projected onto her; she is seen as the cause of it just as she is seen as the cause for libido satisfaction. An ambivalent attitude is thus established toward her; she is alternately "good" and "bad." At weaning time the infant suffers a trauma that has already been described. The nipple as a symbol of the mother is temporarily denied, the infant shows signs of irritation (negative projections onto the mother) and withdraws his love until he can adjust. This is a counterpart of what is seen in the psychotherapeutic situation where, when the trauma of setting the final date occurs, the positive projections are withdrawn and the negative ones reappear until the patient can readjust, that is, overcome his denial. The average infant does promptly overcome the denial, but his subsequent relation to the mother is different because the libido previously satisfied at the breast no longer has this outlet and is displaced downward to the genitalia in the manner already described. The trauma connected with termination of the oral stage and introduction of the narcissistic stage gives rise to a transient denial and slight negative identification. This not only makes the mother responsible for the loss of the previous satisfaction but makes her out as the cause for the restraint of the oral sadismus which arises from this loss and which he fears to express. Here, then, we see an early responsibility to the mother for restraint, which indicates the beginning of a superego.

Negative identification and denial of the anus (toilet training).—Up to this time the whole process has been biological, but with the advent of the mother's training to cleanliness and toilet habits the social influence begins and the child must learn to accept it. As already stated the character of the mother is all-important here. But the negative identification which began with weaning is increased in any case; for the negative reaction to the mother's restraint of the former freedom in regard to urination and defecation is repressed through fear of her authority. Denial of the mother during this period thus adds somewhat to the strength of the superego already begun with the reaction to weaning. And the superego is further strengthened by the negative identification induced by all the other "don'ts" which are implied by the mother's social training: don't make faces, don't stick out your tongue; don't pick your nose; don't use bad, dirty words; don't swear, etc.

The Oedipus situation.—It is apparent then, in recapitulation, that positive identification first modifies the primitive oral libido in the sense of "love"—i.e., sets the mother up as an ideal figure—and that negative identification induced by weaning and toilet training modifies the oral sadismus and diminishes the luster of this ideal by setting her up as a restraining authority. At the time of realization of sex difference and beginning maturation of the sex glands the narcissistic period, which began with weaning, should come to an end and the libido again be projected outward. But the maternal restraints established in the superego stand in the way and this period is often one of great stress. Normal boys often have dreams of intercourse with the mother; that is to say, they overcome this restraint sadistically in fantasy.

In the male the overcoming of this negative identification with the mother is all the more important because she must be the prototype of his sexual partner, with whom a positive identification must be possible. What happens is that the restraints which have hitherto been projected onto her are now shifted to the father, who thus becomes their bearer and toward whom the male feels guilt if he violates the social code in regard to sex. This is evident in the psychotherapeutic situation where, when the patient overcomes his denial of the mother, i.e., accepts the woman as his sexual object, his relation to the therapist becomes that of man to man, and he is really anxious to get away from him. Sometimes this anxiety to get away is so strong that he begs to be excused from the last few sessions. In his role of bearer of the social restraints the father thus becomes the final superego for the man, and the woman his sexual object. But if the man can accept these restraints himself he no longer feels guilty to the father, is independent of him. In the female, on the other hand, the negative identification with the mother remains and the libido is projected onto the father who becomes the prototype of her future mate. This projection, too, becomes evident in the psychotherapeutic situation where the negative identification with the mother results in the same type of complaining of the self and others but particularly of the mother. Gradually she adopts a positive attitude toward the therapist as she identifies positively with him but her denial of the mother can never be wholly overcome for she is the bearer of the original social restraints for the woman. With setting of the final date this denial again blossoms out against the therapist only to recede when the patient partly overcomes it. But at the termination of the psychotherapy she should have the same attitude toward him that she has toward the mother and thus be free to seek a suitable mate. The old restraints formerly projected onto the mother now become her own superego by acceptance of responsibility for them. In the change from the first object relationship in infancy with the mother to the next object relationship at sexual maturity the woman thus changes from the original object to the opposite sex but keeps the original superego, while the man keeps the original sexual object but changes the superego to the opposite sex.

Finally, the average mature adult almost never fully accepts the responsibility for restraint of his libido and sadismus but projects it onto familial, religious, or governmental authorities and then feels guilty when he disregards the rules of conduct laid down by them. But it should be remembered that these rules of conduct stem from man himself, not from a supernatural source; the basis for ethics lies in man's ego structure, which in turn finds an almost exact anatomic counterpart as will be shown in a later chapter.

Pathological Development

In the broadest sense persons with aberrant psychological development who *request* treatment may be divided into two classes: (1) those with average ego structure whose development has been thwarted by unusual maternal environment; and (2) those endowed with an unusual amount of oral sadismus and whose development has been distorted by average maternal environment. Persons endowed with an unusual amount of oral libido do not *request* treatment though they may be at war with all social environment. The first easily recovers under treatment or when removed from the maternal influence; the second presents a problem which can only be resolved properly by understanding the ego structure and the therapeutic principles derived from it.

But no sharp line can be drawn between these two classes. The elements in the ego structure of the first show less strength, those of the second more. And in the experience of the writer this strength is generally manifested by the degree to which the oral sadismus is projected onto the first object, the mother, and by the tenacity with which it maintains this object relationship. This explains the continued denial of the neurotic, the pervert, and the psychotic, since each clings tenaciously to the early mother object.

In the neurotic the fixation at the early stage is not too great; the denial can be overcome by proper treatment. But the reason is that this type of individual has a deepened self-consciousness and therefore suffers intensely from the punishing activity of his superego. The pervert, on the other hand, is much less self-aware, suffers less punishment from his superego, accepts himself as he has become, and therefore does not desire treatments. This can be illustrated by the case of a young male homosexual who consulted the writer with the idea of improving his relations with other persons for business reasons; he would not accept treatment because he feared that his homosexuality might be altered. The psychotic may be favorably affected by treatment when it is possible to establish a personal relationship with him. But this is not usually the case, because all feeling relationship with the object has been denied.

It is now proposed to outline briefly the developmental course of those persons in the second class, i.e., those endowed with an unusual amount of oral sadismus. A great number of these persons will tell the therapist that their complaints date back to their earliest memories or at least that they remember having unusual feelings in relation to the mother at a very early age. However, the recall of these memories of early events is relatively unimportant; what is important is that, under proper conditions, the patient soon reveals the biological level at which his development has been partially arrested and that he reacts to the therapist on this level. Since this arrest not unusually dates back to the weaning period it is important to show the significance of the nipple in genetic psychology.

The Oral Stage

The nipple and mouth as sexual organs.—The nipple is a sexual organ. This fact is shown by its engorgement from stimulation under suitable psychic conditions and by the sexual sensations evoked in the mother during nursing. The mouth, too, must be considered to be connected with sexuality. This is shown by the fact that sexual intercourse is practically always initiated by kissing; indeed, sexual immaturity is often indicated by the way in which the woman receives the kiss.

The first object relationship.—During the nursing period these two sexual organs meet with mutual satisfaction and the first object relationship is established, a purely biological relationship.

Pathology of negative identification.—At weaning time the relationship is broken off; there is denial of the nipple and negative identification with the mother, and the libido is displaced downward in the manner already described. This downward course is shown by transference of the oral libido to the thumb and thence to the genitalia, where a substitute satisfaction is found; during the ensuing narcissistic stage the penis now substitutes for the nipple in the male and the clitoris in the female. But some libido remains in the mouth and hand, particularly in the male, and is manifested in later life by the sexual satisfaction sought in kissing, and in petting the genitalia.

When the amount of oral sadismus is greater than average the denial of the nipple may not be overcome, as in the average case, and so may be continued into adult life. This condition means that the infant's negative expressions continue to be suppressed through fear of the mother, and he installs her as a restraining authority who in this case is more feared than loved. This continued suppression affects the development of the positive side through the ego structure, as already described, and the *degree* to which this development is affected determines to a large extent the fate of the individual. For if the negative identification is very strong the suppression of oral sadismus may be so great as to arrest almost completely the development of positive expression at the oral stage: in adult life a preponderant part of the libido remains in the mouth and hand, instead of being displaced downward to the genitalia. This abnormality does not become so apparent until sexual maturation, when the effect of the maternal restraints makes outward projection of the libido onto a person of the opposite sex more difficult; in the male the female genitalia may then be denied, in the female the male genitalia, and the negative identification still further increased. If a point is reached where the genitalia of the opposite sex are repellent, then the narcissism is continued in the sense that it is projected outward onto a replica of the self, i.e., onto another homosexual.

In the heterosexual male the ego functions mainly through the genitalia, the mouth and hand playing the lesser part; in the homosexual it functions mostly through the mouth and hand, the genitalia playing the lesser part. In this way his mouth becomes a vagina to the other man, so to speak. With this understanding of the development of homosexuality it now becomes clear why the neurotic is in constant fear of homosexuality; he is part way there.

In the heterosexual female at sexual maturation the libido displaced downward to the clitoris to act as a substitute satisfaction for the lost nipple during the narcissistic period must be relocated in her own nipple; this leaves her own vagina free to respond to the stimulation from the penis of her mate. She accomplishes this by relinquishing to the male her own aggressive reaction to the maternal restraints and then identifying positively with him. But this is just what many women do not accomplish. The result again depends on the strength of the maternal restraints. When these are very strong the woman may keep her aggressive reaction to them, maintain her narcissism and her denial of the male genitalia, and project her libido onto a replica of herself, onto another homosexual. But when the maternal restraints and her reaction against them are less strong she may keep some aggressive reaction against them, marry a man less aggressive than she, and produce children; but she is sexually frigid and often unhappy throughout her life because of her preponderantly negative identification with the mother. The orgasm may be achieved but only by masturbation; and her strong maternal restraints prevent this.

Signs of arrest at the oral stage.—The significance of denial of the nipple at weaning is often revealed during therapy. A young woman dreamed before one of the early sessions that she had a loose tooth and that she could not decide whether it should be pulled or left in. Now the appearance of teeth in an infant often helps to decide that nursing should be terminated. This dream indicated that because of the trauma of weaning she had denied the nipple and identified negatively with the mother; for without the tooth she might again have nursed at the breast.

Another patient, a young man who resented his mother, revealed during an early session that he got a great "kick" out of looking at the beautiful busts of young women, but that he felt guilty about doing it. This undue satisfaction in looking at the breast harked back to his oral stage, which he was loath to leave, and indicated that his resentment of the mother stemmed from denial of the nipple and negative identification with her at this early period.

Period of Toilet Training

When the mother has been stern and strict or has even punished for "dirtiness" during the period of toilet training, the whole perineal area may come under the same ban. A child with more than average oral sadismus may then react positively against this negative identification by associating its *libido* with the anus; this is in defiance of the mother.

In the male this may lead to sodomy in adult life if the female genitalia are also denied at the time of sexual maturation.

In the female it may lead to pathological masochism; the woman has a fantasy during masturbation in which the man gives her blows on the buttocks; or during intercourse the man must actually strike her buttocks.

The writer has had a number of patients who dreamed of toilets in connection with young children, indicating denial of the mother at this period. One woman dreamed of urinating and defecating in public: an obvious defiance of the mother.

Advent of a Sibling

The younger sibling is frequently denied because of jealousy. When the older girl denies the younger brother and does not overcome the denial, the result may be disastrous for her. For this negative identification with him accentuates her aggressive reaction against the maternal restraints and makes it very difficult for her to give up her narcissism: her libido therefore remains attached to the clitoris and she is unable to achieve the orgasm during intercourse. The writer has in mind one such woman who married and had a child but gradually became more and more unhappy-looking; now, in middle life, she is a stony-faced, rigid personality who obviously sees the whole outside world through dark glasses. It is not the lack of sexual satisfaction alone that disturbs such a person; her lack of sex life is merely a sign of her persistent negativism and denial of feeling. Such a woman may achieve the orgasm but only by titillating the clitoris, which act the maternal restraints prevent her doing; in her attempts to get sexual satisfaction she will often take the active male position during intercourse, a sure sign of her male identification: she wants to be "on top" and manifests this ideologically by attempting always to show that she is right and the man wrong.

Realization of Sex Difference

When the denial of the mother has been unusually great during the narcissistic period the adult genitalia may be denied at the time of maturation of the sex glands; psychological maturation does not accompany physiological maturation and there is little or perhaps only simulated interest in the opposite sex.

The male is aloof and embarrassed in the presence of normal young women and feels inferior in the presence of riotous young men; he is afraid to look them in the eye and may suspect himself of homosexual tendencies. He masturbates instead of showing interest in the opposite sex and if he brings himself to attempt intercourse he may be impotent. Mothers worry about these boys because they are so different from their fellows and are not interested in girls. It is his continued negative identification with the mother that he cannot overcome and that gives him this "castration complex." His development has been arrested at the "Oedipus stage."

The female shows less obvious signs of her immaturity because for a long time youthful innocence has been cherished in many adult minds; this standard is much less prevalent today than formerly. She may marry without knowledge of sexual intercourse, and without having masturbated, in the belief that babies emerge from the navel or from the rectum. But in the present-day female with a greater amount of oral sadismus than normal she is much more likely to become interested in a business or professional career and so justify her narcissistic masculine complex in competition with men; she calls this a man's world and laughs off sex after a few unsatisfactory experiences with it.

It seems useless to continue further this description of such types. An understanding of the psychological mechanisms makes it clear that early suppression of oral sadismus because of fear of the mother results in strong negative identification with her and that this "maternal restraint" is a very disturbing element in the life of the individual. When it entirely overbalances the positive side and prevents the emergence of the latter toward an ideal, the results are disastrous because of the overpowering feeling of inadequacy, helplessness, and guilt. This may cause the individual to seek relief by such means which stimulate his narcissistic self-love as alcohol and narcotics, or in various types of "badness" which defy the mother, such as molesting young children. The varieties of such behavior are endless.

The Creative Type

But when the degree of negative identification is only moderate the individual may justify himself by creativity. It is a well-known fact that the sex life of some creative artists has been aberrant. The writer once heard a bisexual artist justify himself by saying that some of the great spirits had been homosexuals. His ego structure was flexible enough to allow him to play the mother to a homosexual on the oral stage at one time and the "bad" son to the mother substitute, his wife, at another.

Again, the artist may establish and pursue an ideal of creativity in literature, art, or music in spite of his sex deficiency and so, to the extent that he obtains recognition, justify himself. However, this justification is a compulsive effort to overcome the maternal restraints and is often accomplished as such cost as to destroy the ego structure sooner or later. Or he may throw off the maternal restraints entirely at puberty by the establishment of an individual ideal of creativity and lead a normal and sometimes a very free and happy sex life by completely disregarding the usual social restraints in regard to it. But this requires a compensatory denial of his superego through "sadismus" which justifies his individual sex ideal.

Psychological Aberrations

Psychosomatic disease.—Another way in which the ego may justify itself in spite of this negative identification with the mother is by downward projection of the restraint. The mechanism by which this occurs will become clear after consideration of the anatomic counterpart of the ego structure. But it may be stated here that anatomic connections exist by means of which this downward projection out of the ego structure and into the soma may take place. Thus many types of gastrointestinal disease and functional disturbances of the sex apparatus and urinary tract may be explained. To this must be added the premature aging of joints, muscles, etc., which follows the continual fatigue incident to this downward projection of the maternal restraints.

Phobias.—It has been noted that when the maternal restraints have been great and the negative identification very strong, the individual is almost helpless to act effectively and has a very "blue" outlook on the world. This state may lead to specific acts by which he seeks to avoid the unhappy consequences of his denial. Thus when the female genitalia have been denied at the Oedipus stage the victim may consciously avoid the presence and even the sight of women because they bring on thoughts of his inadequacy and unhappiness. Or when the outlook is so gloomy as to bring on thoughts of self-destruction he may consciously avoid even passing a place associated with death. Thus an undertaker once treated for a hysterical neurosis had a well-marked phobia in which he tried to avoid even passing a hospital because this brought on severe pains down his left arm.

The compulsion neurosis.—This aberration which Rank called the commonest neurosis of our time represents a desperate attempt to overcome the negative identification by force. Most often the compulsion is to thought, and the individual is tortured by fantasies which are an expression of his revolt against the intolerable restraint under which he labors; they are therefore negative in character. Occasionally the compulsion is so strong as to force action. Thus a man was once seen to arise in church, rush forward, and begin to declaim that religion was all wrong before he was seized by members of the congregation. It is obvious that this was a compulsive protest against his own restraints which he attempted to overcome by acting in this way: religion was a form of restraint and therefore all wrong.

But in the creative individual the compulsion toward thought may alternate between the positive and pleasant and the negative and unpleasant. The positive fantasies are often sexual in nature and have a somewhat sadistic trend in so far as they entirely ignore the wishes of the other party; but they are invariably followed by others which are negative and painful because they portray the individual as helpless, inadequate, and guilty. If the compulsion succeeds in forcing the individual into action he may make "love" to his object but the affair is usually abortive because of his succeeding phase of helplessness, inadequacy, and guilt.

Egoism.—Egoism is a very common consequence of early denial of the mother. When this denial is continued after weaning but the negative reaction to it finds some expression instead of being completely suppressed by fear during the ensuing narcissistic period it may be partly overcome at the time of sexual maturation. The individual is potent but incapable of positive identification with the woman and therefore of love. But the increased narcissism makes him increasingly sensitive; he has denied an outer reality, the nipple that formerly gave him satisfaction, and this has acted through the ego structure to impede but not to arrest the development of his libido, which is left crude and sadistic as it was in the adolescent period. He is incapable of true feeling. The slightest blow to his self-love, his vanity, makes him try to defend himself by increasing his narcissism; this in turn makes him even more vulnerable. If his biological self is stronger than his social self this egoism may result in a Don Juan complex. Some of the maternal restraints may be evidenced in his toilet habits but his sexuality entirely escapes them. He has affairs with one girl after another but each ends because he grows tired of her or she of him and his irresponsible ego. His sex life is rationalized as love without a positive identification. If he has to marry because of an accidental pregnancy he continues his philandering and fails to assume responsibility for the wife and child. His basic negativism toward the mother may be manifested toward the mother substitutes throughout his entire life.

Anxiety neurosis.—Casual observation of an infant shows that fear plays a considerable part in its natural endowment as soon as it becomes at all familiar with its surroundings : fear of a strange face, fear of being left alone, etc. In other words, fear does not arise from an outside source but is latent in the individual. When positive identification with the mother has occurred, this fear is connected with separation from her. After the transient denial of weaning and resumption of a happy relationship with her it gradually diminishes as the infant identifies positively with such other persons as playmates and teachers.

But when the trauma of weaning is great and a strong negative identification with the mother takes place the fear is not overcome and may persist during adolescence and into adult life. Such an adult fears almost every new experience; the fear may dominate him to such an extent that he stays in his room most of the time. This may be illustrated by the case of an almost moronic young woman treated by the writer some years ago. Following an unhappy maternal relationship and childhood she became a juvenile delinquent and had unsatisfactory sex experiences; finally she limited her activity to the simplest routine, which centered about her own room. During treatment it was possible for her to overcome her negative identification with the mother and the world, and at its termination she got a job as a maid in a hotel.

During the adolescent period she had attempted unsuccessfully to overcome the maternal restraints by seeking narcissistic satisfactions. But her fear had gradually surmounted everything else and prevented pursuit of further experiences. It was salutary in the sense that it was a recognition of an inner reality.

Hysterical neurosis.—This is usually characterized by emotional outbursts which are justified by simulated organic disease. The former are manifestations of suffering and must be understood as directed against the restraints resulting from negative identification with the mother; the latter may be downward projections into the soma by way of the autonomic system or may affect the cortex so as to cause paralyses or anesthesias. A single woman was referred to the writer by a urologist some years ago. She complained of frequency and urgency of urination for which he could find no cause at all. And her disability was so great as to hospitalize her at times. It is now obvious to the writer that the symptoms were a protest against a negative identification with the mother, who was thus made out to be the cause of all her suffering. This identification must have arisen at the time of toilet training, when the whole perineal area came under the ban of "dirtiness"; the symptoms were a childlike protest against the mother's commands, a form of "badness" by which the patient showed defiance. Bed-wetting is a similar protest in boys.

Obsessional neurosis.—This is often connected with sexuality, the complaint then being of an almost constant preoccupation with sexual matters. Here again the neurosis dates back to the early period of toilet training, when the mother has been stern and strict, or perhaps to the time of infantile masturbation, which she has interdicted. The preoccupation is a form of "badness," a way of asserting that the individual will do as he pleases and not as the mother pleases. Some years ago the author saw a single male patient who complained of just such a preoccupation. He was quite morose about his condition, evidently because of a feeling of guilt toward the mother. One thing that particularly disturbed him was the idea that a woman's labia were pressed against his forehead. He was potent and had often tried to get free of his complaint by having sexual intercourse with a prostitute. However, this gave him only temporary relief.

The psychoses.—In the perversions and psychoses the mechanism of projection is used to a greater extent than in the psychoneuroses and the fixation to the object by identification is therefore greater. In the psychoses this fixation is less open to study because these patients do not have the "object hunger" shown by the neurotic; they do not seek treatment but have it thrust upon them. Nevertheless some begin to react almost at once to therapy. And this reaction seems to be one of gratitude because the therapist shows understanding instead of superiority.

But the mechanism of denial plays the most prominent part in the development of the psychoses. The denial is not so much of an outer reality such as occurs in normal development—denial of the mother as a libidinous object during the narcissistic period—but more of an inner reality, the reality of the feeling relationship to her. This denial of feeling has been described as a transient withdrawal of positive projections onto the object; if it is extended to include as well a withdrawal of negative projections onto the mother, then all affective relations to her are denied. She can no longer give the individual pain and disillusionment because he is entirely indifferent to her. But since the mother constitutes the first reality for the child the denial comes eventually to mean the absence of all affective relations to the outer

world. This is what is found in schizophrenia. But the denial merely emphasizes the strength of the original projections. The schizophrenic has identified almost completely with the mother object, positively and negatively,
that is to say, withdrawn both projections. However, the forces which would
otherwise have been projected outward to establish a feeling relationship
with the outer world still exist in a primitive form; sooner or later they
appear as behavior that differs from that of the schizophrenic's superficial
character and emphasizes the fact that his social self and his biological self
are divergent and primitive. This behavior shows three trends that are
roughly similar to those of the so-called normal: a crudely positive libidinous
trend, often at the oral stage, which is projected outward onto fancied objects; a crudely negative sadistic trend, also projected outward; and a painful
masochistic trend which turns inward as self-punishment. These are often
displayed in wonderful imagery and with extraordinary facial expressions
that indicate the unusual strength of the primitive forces.

The paranoiac, on the other hand, has denied all feeling relationship to
the mother, that is, permanently withdrawn the positive projections, but
projected the pain and hatred that resulted from his disillusionment with
her outward onto the object; it is now the outer world that hates and perse-
cutes him as the mother formerly did. And he compensates this to some
extent by delusions of grandeur, that is, by narcissistic reinforcement of his
biological self.

If the schizophrenic and paranoiac do not readily offer their structures
for study the manic-depressive does; he seems to lie on the border between
psychosis and neurosis. Indeed, minor variations of this type are often found
in so-called normal persons as cyclic variations of mood. The manic-depressive is primarily sadistic as well as egoistic; unlike the neurotic he tends to
act out his impulses instead of reflecting on them. Since he has not overcome his first denial of the mother he projects his hatred onto her substitutes
and so is incapable of love; his sex life is purely sensual. The cyclic character
of his emotional life is due to the fact that he overcomes the maternal restraints in his superego while he is in the manic phase and then is overcome
by them in the depressive phase. Finally he may reach a stage of melancholia
in which he sees that his manic activity is "bad" and hates himself.

The sado-masochistic mechanism.—In the section on normal development the mechanism by which primitive oral libido is modified at its source
was elucidated: under the beneficent influence of positive identification with
the mother the oral sadismus dams back to restrain the primitive oral libido
at its source. But when the first object relationship with the mother is terminated at weaning the denial of the nipple may be maintained. This results
in a permanent withdrawal of the positive projection and a negative identification with her. Thus instead of *development* of the primitive libido we find

it to be *arrested* at the oral stage. Such an arrested development is usual in neurotics. Off and on a fairly free expression of oral sadismus may be projected onto the mother but because of the negative identification with her the ensuing guilt feeling is also projected onto her. The result is that the patient's expression shows sadistic episodes and that these are followed by periods of guilty submission during which he berates, belittles, or punishes himself in one way or another, i.e., is masochistic. This reciprocal interplay of sadistic expression and masochistic self-punishment Rank has called the sado-masochistic mechanism. It may easily be seen and studied in all neurotic patients, for like the psychic mechanisms it is acted out on the therapist. A neurotic woman after a long recital of her suffering paused and looked expectantly at the therapist; what she really wanted was evidence of sympathy on his part. When this was not forthcoming there was a slight stiffening in her attitude; she grew quite irritated at him and seemed about to decide against further treatment. When asked at the conclusion of the session if she wished to come again she hesitated for a few moments before answering and then responded with a doubtful "yes." She thus demonstrated the operation of the sado-masochistic mechanism in her relation to the therapist, but in reverse.

The sado-masochistic mechanism is evidently the basis for the cyclic changes seen in the manic-depressive type, where the sex life may be very active during the manic phase but nonexistent in the depressive phase, when, indeed, all forms of activity seem to be almost arrested at their very source. This indicates to the present writer that this type of behavior is partially fixed in the character and that the cycles operate through the id so as to permit unrestricted expression of primitive sadistic libido or completely to arrest almost all activity.

The difference found between the manic-depressive type and the neurotic type arises from the fact that in the former the biological self, in the latter the social self is the stronger. The neurotic type reflects first and then cannot act; the manic-depressive type acts first and then cannot escape his own self-punishment.

The id.—Libido is recognized in adult life as sexual desire, but the term evidently has been given a much more generic meaning, for the pleasure the infant finds at the breast has been accepted as oral libido. The present writer gives it a still broader meaning and defines it not only as the force which makes the infant cling to the mother, which draws two lovers together, which makes man gregarious, but also as the force found in other mammals, and even in lower vertebrates, such as birds and fishes, which impels them to return to their place of origin year after year for mating or ovulation. It would thus culminate in sexuality but not be necessarily connected with it, particularly in man, in whom through thousands of years of sublimation it would have resulted in all his finer feelings. Since it appears at a stage when consciousness can be said to be almost entirely without content and when the peripheral nervous system and sex glands are undeveloped, this elemental human satisfaction must arise from the very core of the central nervous system. Doubtless it was this consideration which led Freud to give it the importance that he did. Since it can find expression only through action of one kind or another, any consideration of its source must also involve that of action. Freud saw this source as a structure located at an instinctual level beneath consciousness and named it the id. The preceding discussion of modification or arrest of primitive libidinous activity at its source in the id brings this structure into relation with both of the forces which are projected onto the therapist in the psychotherapeutic situation. These were conceived by the present writer as arising from actual nuclei in the ego structure and projected back to their earliest beginnings as oral sadismus and oral libido in Rank's genetic psychology. As the oral sadismus dams back under the influence of the mother's love its direction changes : instead of being projected outward in sadistic expression it turns into the ego structure to act on, i.e., to restrain and modify the primitive libido. This implies actual connections between the nucleus from which the oral sadismus emanates and the structural id from which the activity of the primitive libido arises. These structural connections have already been indicated, but their final elucidation must await demonstration in their anatomic counterpart.

V

RANK'S WILL PSYCHOLOGY[1]

The will has long been considered to be the source of man's spiritual difficulties, as the ancient argument about freedom of the will plainly shows; for bad will tends to germinate guilt, which in turn prevents the will from being really free. In this materialistic era philosophical thinking is often labeled unscientific, doubtless as a reaction to the religious connotations of the term "will," and to the closed mind which often accompanies religious dogma. But the present failure of religion to solve the problems of the mind should not blind us to the significance of religious and philosophic thinking. For religion is only a projection of man's responsibility onto a supernatural moral authority, and the two main problems of philosophy, ethics, and the determination of man's relation to reality are essentially those of psychotherapy.

It was doubtless these considerations which led Rank to found his will psychology on the principles described in his genetic psychology but more or less to abandon his previous "psychoanalytic" terminology. For "bad" will and "good" will are obviously the same psychic forces we have described from their first beginnings as oral sadismus and oral libido. This change relates his psychology to a wealth of cultural-historical material and not only makes it transcend the narrower problems of psychoneurosis and psychosis, but makes the knowledge gained through their understanding applicable to religion and philosophy.

The will.—The will uses libido for its own purposes and is a much more general principle of life and action. Since Rank saw the will as arising in the id and gave it the importance in the biological self which Freud attributed to libido, the view that both arise from a common source in the id, and that libido is a subsidiary of the will, seems to the present writer to represent more fully the biological self. In a sense this view unites those of both Freud and Rank.

The opposing will.—In Rank's will psychology the psychic principle which is seen as cruelty or negative projection and changes into restraint of primitive libido in the psychotherapeutic situation becomes the opposing will. This is more than a mere change of terminology. For introduction of the term "opposing will" gives a certain autonomy to this restraint just as substitution of the word "will" for "libido" gives autonomy to the biological

[1] See *Truth and Reality,* and *Will Therapy* (New York: Alfred A. Knopf, Inc., 1936).

33

self. Furthermore, the introduction of the idea of the opposing will as a part of the ego structure takes the concept of a social self as a restraining force out of the realm of the supernatural and brings it down to earth: it makes man's ethical values and religions understandable as a development of his own structure; it makes restraint an actual physiological force which, together with the will, is able to externalize itself by projection and to take the outer into the inner world by identification. This identification is facilitated by the firm connections with outer reality that Rank gives the opposing will through the visual and auditory sensory apparatus.

Will and opposing will both expressed together in behavior.—Social self and biological self, oral sadismus and oral libido, opposing will and will, have been described as separate forces which contributed to the formation of personality. But these forces find expression *together* in a common medium which we call behavior and recognize in general attitude, facial expression, voice, and action. If there were such a thing as a perfectly integrated person we would not find it possible to separate these elements in his behavior. But in the best of persons this is far from true. For he has moods which indicate that from one day to another, even from one hour to another, one force or the other predominates. In the aberrations, in psychoneurosis and psychosis, these phases are so marked as to influence the behavior and make this predominance evident to an astute observer. In the fields of mental aberration, just as in the field of somatic pathology it is the abnormal which makes it possible to understand the normal.

Content of the will.—It seems important to the present writer to emphasize that the terms "will" and "opposing will" are abstractions; they refer to the general principles behind the content; they interpret the nature of the principle from the context in which the content is used. For man ordinarily thinks in terms of content, not will. He desires beautiful women, more luxurious surroundings, swifter automobiles, without realizing that the satisfaction he attains through them is more due to achievement of his will than to its particular content. In the same way the negative quality of the opposing will may find any number of different contents, may be rationalized in a thousand different ways. Much of our "thought" is made up of this intellectualized negativism. In order to see the patient as he really is the therapist must be able to get behind all this window dressing which is skillfully used to disguise the real meaning. And here is where the real art of interpretation begins; it is only by interpretation that we are able to thread a path through the mass of projections, rationalizations, and denials that go by the name of thought.

The realm of feeling.—The will arises in the id but does not become conscious till it reaches the realm of feeling, where its content is evaluated by its feeling quality. Thus a libidinous content is given the will in the autoerotic narcissistic stage of adolescence and young manhood, is recognized in the realm of feeling, and immediately projected onto an object. This is not always at hand but the human being is able to circumvent this difficulty easily because he has an inner projection field to which a suitable object from past experience may be recalled and projected into consciousness, brought out from a storehouse, and used again. This allows him to act inwardly as well as outwardly. He can project himself and his object into this field of consciousness and even visualize a complete series of actions on his part and reactions on the part of the object. And this inner projection gives him time to reflect. The man of action tends to do less of this; his inner projection field tends to rationalize his will more easily. The man of thought tends to do more; his action time is delayed and his inner projection field more under the influence of the restraint from his superego.

The opposing will, too, becomes conscious in this region as a feeling of opposition. The neurotic soon becomes aware of this opposition because its force is great in him. It seeks to find expression in the psychotherapeutic situation and the resentment which he has harbored is thus verbalized. But the opposing will has an inner projection field as does the will, though its use has often been prevented by the superego. The neurotic not only fears to express hostile thoughts but he fears to think them because of the punishing authority of the superego. In the psychotherapeutic situation he overcomes this fear sufficiently to verbalize and finally even to think hostile thoughts, i.e., to project them into consciousness, because he projects the responsibility onto the therapist, makes him his temporary superego. The opposing will, like the conscious will, thus seems to have a certain autonomy in the ego, for the individual now has some choice as to whether to verbalize or to think these thoughts. Not only that, but as he identifies positively with the therapist, the negative thoughts dam back and thus seem to act through the id to modify the primitive character of the will and libido as previously described. To the extent that this material has not previously been expressed and now appears, it represents the "unconscious" discovered by Freud. Since the superego either prevents the projection of hostile thoughts into consciousness or punishes for them after their projection it must be connected with consciousness as apart from the opposing will, and since it may be projected onto the therapist it evidently must have originated from projection in the first place, first onto the mother, later onto the father, and finally onto the therapist. Furthermore, since its punishing effects tend to disappear during psychotherapy these effects must be "learned" from previous experiences though this does not necessarily imply severity on the part of the mother. And since fear of the superego prevents expression of the conscious will, connections must exist in the realm of feeling between the conscious will and opposing will, but also between the conscious will and its conscious aim on the one hand and the opposing will and the conscious superego on the other.

Formation of ideals.—During the autoerotic stage of man, late adolescence and early manhood, his ideal seems to be woman; she takes first place in this inner projection field. But as he satisfies his sexual and spiritual needs in marriage and develops further, his ideal changes according to his type. By identification the average man takes his ideal together with his character from those about him and competes with them according to the strength of his will. The creative man whose conscious will is stronger than his opposing will, the man of action, creates his own ideal partly from persons he sees and reads about, partly from his own spiritual necessities, but struggles to attain them in the outer world, externalizes and makes his conflict objective. The creative man whose opposing will is stronger than his conscious will, the man of thought, forms his ideal similarly to solve his individual problem; but the inner conflict is externalized in the field of art, literature, or philosophy where his production, his work, represents his solution. The neurotic, as a man of thought, is also creative. But instead of forming the ideal which his individualism requires, he accepts that of the average man about him. His opposing will turns into the ego structure at an early stage to restrain the developing will because he fears to give it expression. The psychotherapeutic problem is thus to help him give expression to his opposing will and so allow his will to develop and to form and seek its own ideal. It becomes apparent in the psychotherapeutic situation, where this development may be watched, that what Freud called the "unconscious" represents in part the stages through which the will passes.

Integration.—The aim of the creative personality of the man of thought, for it is with him that we are presently concerned, is integration of his ideals with the ethical principles of his superego. This means that the experiences accumulated since birth will have been evaluated and sifted by his ethical superego and then stored away in suitable categories as character. His character, the product of his will and opposing will, will be a structure representing the results of his struggle to maintain his own inner truth against outer reality.

Consciousness.—The reader may now see that consciousness in the sense used here is represented in the main by the two inner projection fields just described; it is in them that we "think." But it must be remembered that in the average person the inner projection field of the opposing will is almost completely dominated by the individual's superego, which prevents most of the expression of his opposing will. It and the attached superego lie not in the realm of consciousness but in the "unconscious." And when the neurotic applies for therapy it is often found that his opposing will has been similarly dominated by his superego and therefore lies in the "unconscious." He may tell his story for an hour or so and then gradually come to a halt. Only when he finds that the therapist is not pressing him to talk and explains that if he desires to be silent that is just as important as his speech, does his opposing will really begin to find expression. The therapist on the other hand must have passed through the stage of expression of the opposing will and have experienced its damming back with the establishment of his own ideals to be able to recognize what is going on in his patients. Consciousness in the sense of the site where thought goes on in most persons must then be considered to lie in the inner projection field of the conscious will.

To the site of consciousness must be added the fields onto which the visual and auditory stimuli are projected and from which the images and sounds recorded must be projected outward. For it seems to the present writer indubitable that the ego participates in the seeing and hearing process and that *it* is the force which projects the images to the eyes and ears from the cortex where they are interpreted and registered. Further consideration makes it seem likely that it is the opposing will to which these images are passively transmitted (its connections with outer reality) but that the will may at times participate when an effort is made to pay particular attention to what is seen or heard. For seeing and hearing may be active or passive depending on the momentary aim of the will.

From the fact that in the newborn infant consciousness appears to be quite without content one must surmise that content is gradually and passively acquired through the eyes, ears, and opposing will until the child shows purpose, when the conscious will participates. Later on memories of past events may be recalled by the conscious will and projected into consciousness, and must therefore have been stored away meanwhile. The will and opposing will would thus learn to deal with content as well as feeling.

The dream.—There is no part of the psychotherapeutic situation where the principles of the will psychology outlined above find clearer expression than in the dream. For here the incoming stream of sensory impressions from the eyes and ears has ceased to flow. It is therefore a truly creative expression of the will and opposing will in which the storehouse of memories is freely used to supply the characters. The meaning is concealed by the same kind of ostrich strategy represented by denial and expressed in the inner projection fields of consciousness. Here the biological self is often not only revealed in its primitive, immature form, but the progress that occurs during treatment appears with crystal clarity. In a scene between man and woman, for example, where sexual activity was disguised as a medical procedure, the penis represented by an instrument, and the vagina by the patient's mouth, the dream revealed that her development had been partly arrested at the oral stage. In another case a young man dreamed that he and his half brother and the therapist were in a room; the half brother was gravely ill and asked the patient to tell him a funny story to make him feel better, but the half brother died and the patient then locked himself in a closet. Here again each young man represented a different part of the personality: the sick half brother represented the conflict between the opposing will and superego, the one with the funny story the primitive, immature will, and the closet episode the denial.

The will psychology with its separation of the personality into its various elements—id, libido, conscious will, opposing will, superego, ideals, and character—with its connections between these structures and the motor cortex which gives them expression, and with the incoming stream of sensory impressions from the eyes and ears, thus affords an explanation for all the human variations in terms which it is now proposed to present in diagrammatic form as the ego structure.

VI

THE EGO STRUCTURE

The possibility of making the ego structure diagrammatic first developed from a visualization of the conscious will and opposing will as two nuclei with communications permitting one to influence or attempt to dominate the other. This is illustrated in Figure 1, where the principle is applied to the average man, the creative man of action, the creative man of thought, and the neurotic.

These nuclei were then enclosed in a structure called the realm of feeling and the outward projection of these two forces together in the will illustrated as in Figure 2-A. It is understood, of course, that the projection is to the motor cortex through which the will must operate. For it is through the motor cortex that the will finds expression in attitude, facial expression, speech, and action. To this was then added the subconscious id with its appended libido as in Figure 2-B. Following this came the inner projection fields with termination of the conscious will in the ideal structure and of the opposing will in the superego. The ideal structure and the superego together make up the greater portion of consciousness. This is illustrated in Figure 2-C. Then the structure called character was appended to the opposing will as in Figure 2-D, and finally the incoming stream of sensory impressions from the outer world to the opposing will through the eyes and ears as in Figure 2-E.

With this diagram of the ego structure in mind it will now be possible to illustrate some of the situations in the psychotherapeutic situation so as to show in a clearer way what is meant by the psychic mechanisms and by the sado-masochistic mechanism. We may take the case of an average neurotic man who begins a long recital of complaints, first about himself and then about others, and illustrate it with a series of diagrams as in Figure 3. His object hunger, his craving for a relationship, is shown in Figure 3-A by the heavy black line from the sense organs to the opposing will, the punishing action of his superego, which makes him feel guilty and inferior and makes him complain about himself, by the heavy black line from the superego to the opposing will. The passive, self-contained status of the therapist is indicated by the heavy black line from his conscious will to his ideal structure. He is not projecting his will outward to help the patient; he is truly passive but his positive attitude is apparent to the patient. As soon as the latter begins to project his superego onto the therapist and finds no criticism or interpretation of his negative projections they develop rapidly until he finds

FIG. 1
BEGINNING OF THE EGO STRUCTURE

The two main forces in the Psyche visualized as nuclei; each may influence or dominate the other. In genetic psychology the social self becomes "oral sadismus", the biological self "oral libido"; in will psychology the social self becomes opposing will, the biological self conscious will. When one predominates it is shown overpassing the broken line.

AVERAGE MAN

social
self

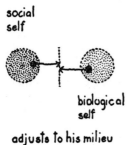

biological
self

adjusts to his milieu

CREATIVE MAN OF ACTION

social
self

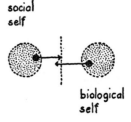

biological
self

overcomes restraints of negative identification
by trial and error in action

NEUROTIC MAN

social
self

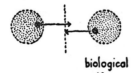

biological
self

negative identification
overcomes biological self

CREATIVE MAN OF THOUGHT

social
self

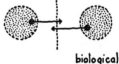

biological
self

overcomes restraints of negative identification
by trial and error in thought

40

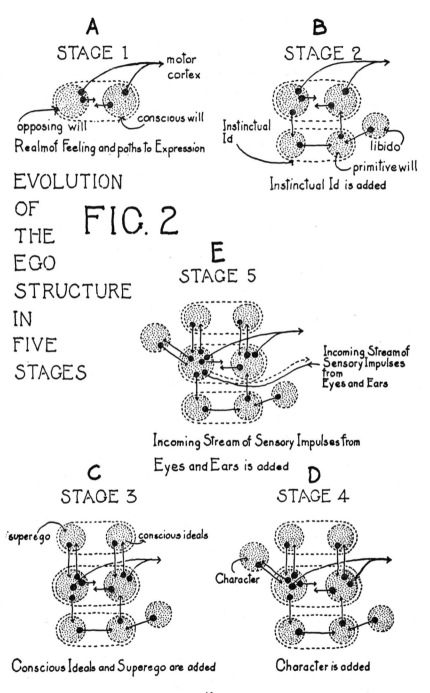

A

STAGE 1

motor cortex

opposing will

conscious will

Realm of Feeling and paths to Expression

B

STAGE 2

Instinctual Id

libido

primitive will

Instinctual Id is added

EVOLUTION OF THE EGO STRUCTURE IN FIVE STAGES

FIG. 2

E

STAGE 5

Incoming Stream of Sensory Impulses from Eyes and Ears

Incoming Stream of Sensory Impulses from Eyes and Ears is added

C

STAGE 3

superego

conscious ideals

Conscious Ideals and Superego are added

D

STAGE 4

Character

Character is added

41

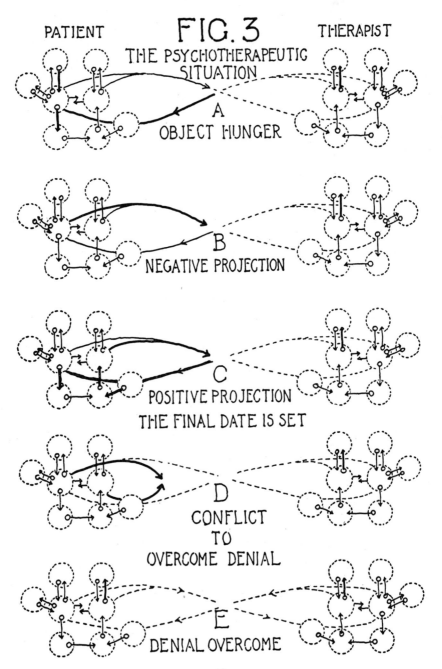

PATIENT FIG. 3 THERAPIST

THE PSYCHOTHERAPEUTIC
SITUATION

A

OBJECT HUNGER

B

NEGATIVE PROJECTION

C

POSITIVE PROJECTION
THE FINAL DATE IS SET

D

CONFLICT
TO
OVERCOME DENIAL

E

DENIAL OVERCOME

42

nothing further to complain about. These negative projections are indicated by the heavy black line going out from the opposing will to the motor cortex in Figure 3-B. Long periods of silence indicate that the patient will soon begin to project positively because his negativisms have been accepted without criticism. Then the negative projections disappear and the primitive will expressions which have been surmised from a few inadvertent remarks are replaced by positive expressions and a generally positive attitude, illustrated in Figure 3-C by the heavy black line going out from the conscious will to the motor cortex. At this stage of therapy the patient is identifying positively with the therapist, as is illustrated by the heavy line from the sense organs to the opposing will in Figure 3-C. At the same time the negative expression from the opposing will has dammed back and acted to restrain and modify the primitive will through the id. This is illustrated in Figure 3-C by the heavy black line from the opposing will to the id.

This shift from negative to positive may occur within the first few sessions, if the therapist does not attack the negative expressions by interpretation, and really marks the beginning of growth. The signs indicate that the patient has now projected his superego onto the therapist, made him the authority. The former now finds interpretation of his primitive infantile attitude, shown in the dreams, but this attitude is explained as a developmental process and since the therapist knows that he himself has gone through the same process at an earlier period his own positive attitude shows understanding, not superiority. He is able to point out, for example, that a dream indicating an oral-genital relationship shows not latent homosexuality but reversion to the primitive oral stage of the first object relationship, in which the mouth and nipple are the sexual organs. In this way the therapist avoids criticism of the present and advice about the future, but the patient cannot fail to connect his guilt feeling with the evidence of his primitive status.

The dreams do not always indicate this infantile status but deal instead with general tendencies which are better interpreted by the will psychology. One comes to understand that the details of genetic psychology, while important for development of the therapist's understanding, are less so for the patient. What *is* important for him is his positive and negative reactions to the therapist and his denial of one or the other of these. The dreams may take an infantile pattern but this is only one way of expressing the reactions, just as a young man may express his love for a girl in his attitude, facial expression, speech, or action. The dream gives content to the positive expression but one must be able to see behind this content to determine the nature of the will expression.

After the date for termination of treatments has been set, the patient projects negatively again onto the therapist as his denial again becomes active (see Fig. 3-D). At this crucial time the therapist must point out that the cause of the patient's conflict is the denial by the will of the feeling relationship to the therapist; the opposing will reappears as opposition but this time as opposition to the patient's own feeling. This fact now demonstrates that the conflict is within the patient. When he overcomes the denial he no longer needs the positive attitude of the therapist because he has established his own ideal (see Fig. 3-E).

The sado-masochistic mechanism.—It is now possible to see what is meant by the sado-masochistic mechanism or, in religious terms, sin and guilt. The negative projections illustrated in Figure 3-B are mildly hostile but nevertheless primitive and cruel in nature; they have heretofore been harbored as a vague resentment and never freely expressed because of the punishing authority of the superego. It is this relation between sadistic expression and masochistic self-punishment that constitutes the sado-masochistic mechanism, in other words, sin and guilt. But it must be borne in mind here that we are using the neurotic, the restrained man of thought, as an example; to him thought and action, when negative, have always been equally sinful. In the psychotherapeutic situation where he projects his superego onto the therapist and finds his negativisms accepted, he expresses this "evil" will freely, can be almost said to exhaust its possibilities; it then begins to dam back and he projects positively. After the final date is set, his struggle is to overcome the necessity of positive identification with the therapist and accept the responsibility for control of his cruelty himself. He succeeds by reason of the ethical demands of his superego which are above and beyond those of his environment and thus spiritual, but also by reason of the formation of ideals toward which he strives, as illustrated in Figure 3-D.

The secret of human behavior.—It is also possible to see in terms of the will psychology that the whole secret of human behavior lies in the relation between the will and opposing will and that this is determined by the denial mechanism. For anger and hatred toward the object originate in the opposing will, which denies the feeling content of the will and attempts to justify itself by outside circumstances. In the average person this denial is followed by remorse, which is a self-punishment inflicted by one's conscience (the superego) and in turn by an access of feeling toward the object which makes amends for the untoward expression of anger and hatred. But if the anger be harbored as righteous and the denial of feeling maintained, the whole psychic economy is disturbed. When this denial is maintained from infancy on, the results may be catastrophic and serious consequences result: the will clings to a primitive oral stage of infantile satisfaction because the ill will toward the mother is suppressed by the superego and acts through the ego structure to arrest the development of the primitive will.

Denial and outer reality.—This form of denial is most apparent in the homosexual, for whom the female genitalia as later representatives of the nipple are completely denied in consciousness. In their place he projects a replica of his own genitalia and thus maintains his narcissistic status. This creates a scotoma (blind spot) in consciousness which disturbs his whole relation to outer reality because so large a part of it is denied in the opposite sex. His secret negativism is intellectually rationalized but his will is constantly forced to maintain the denial of a reality which reaches him through connections between the opposing will and the outer world. He may be intellectually brilliant but his judgment about fundamentals will be faulty.

Creativity.—In the creative person, and to a lesser extent in the average person, the conscious will reacts creatively against the opposing will, particularly in the earlier portion of his life, by an overestimation of reality. An illustration is the type of young man who has a Don Juan complex, whose biological self is stronger than his social self. His conscious will reacts creatively though antisocially against his opposing will; that is, he denies the opposing will and with it all responsibility for the harm he may do his victims. First he rationalizes his conscious will creatively by "loving" them, but this is a rationalization only of libido and not a manifestation of true feeling; the egoist is incapable of that. Then his opposing will forces him to doubt the reality of his "love" and the whole process is repeated. This creativity is apparent in the psychotherapeutic situation, too, when the projections have become positive and pervaded with false optimism, to which the neurotic as an immature person is prone (Fig. 3-C). The satisfaction connected with such a development is projected onto the therapist to whom, in his role of mother, most of the "good" things are attributed. It is this overestimation of reality which makes the average person idealize his love object (in the beginning). And it is the same creative overestimation of reality, that is, a denial of reality, which, by denying the opposing will and its hypothetical connections with the eyes and ears, gives rise to "miracles." They are the counterpart of the hallucinations of the psychotic which would be the negative projections of the opposing will through these same hypothetical connections. Only when an individual can justify his creative denial of the opposing will by actual accomplishment does he become truly creative, and it seems obvious that this sort of justification is what has formed the modern world in which we now live.

The whole complex of psychic mechanisms may be illustrated easily in a family of young children. Let us take, for example, that of a young couple with two children, one a girl of six, the other a girl of three. The older child is extremely intelligent, strong-willed, restrained, and alert to her surroundings; the younger is in some ways more appealing because she reacts more instinctively, but has less intellectual power. Both are well adjusted for their ages. The younger one has been a problem for the older because of her appeal and because the parents' affection naturally must be shared with her, giving the older one somewhat less of it. She reacts perfectly normally in school and when alone with her parents. But occasionally when the younger one is about she will act in this way: she becomes irritable with the younger one (projects negatively onto her) and takes on her whiny, complaining tone of voice (negative identification). She is jealous of the younger sister's charm because she does not possess it, is irritable to her, and then acts like her, i.e., momentarily denies her existence by taking her place. This combination constitutes the denial mechanism. With this child it is not maintained and is soon overcome. But one can see that were this applied to a younger brother and maintained it might cause a male identification with serious later possibilities. In fact the present writer has in mind just such a situation, where the older sister's whole life development has been disturbed by identification with a younger brother. She is now in middle life, a wooden-faced, unhappy, brittle woman who without any doubt is frigid. She could not accept the reality of the existence of the younger brother, denied it, and then identified with him. And it is noteworthy that she is more masculine in type than he.

Understanding of the diagrams in Figure 3 illustrating the psychotherapeutic situation throws much light on the difference between social intercourse and a more intimate family relationship. At the termination of therapy the neurotic is fairly self-contained, like the therapist; his will and opposing will appear together as strength of personality in social intercourse; freer projection of his will and opposing will—that is, of his real self—is reserved for the intimate relationship he may establish later with a sexual partner, with whom, if there be love on the one hand, there most likely will be some irritation and complaining on the other. In this sense the lines indicating projection of the will and opposing will would apply only to the intimate relationship. But the neurotic tends either to lock up or deny all expressions of his will inside of himself through fear, or else to project his real self and its problems onto a chance acquaintance and so become a social nuisance: his "object hunger" exhausts his listener. As a third alternative he projects his problem downward into the psychosomatic realm and, by justifying it with an "illness," makes himself a medical nuisance.

Here then we have a diagram of the ego structure which illustrates the relation of the social to the biological self by hypothetical nuclei and tracts in three levels: (1) an instinctive level below consciousness, (2) a feeling level, and (3) a conscious level. The material or content of "consciousness" is found in the conscious and feeling levels. The diagram affords an explanation for man's historical and individual development as well as the infinite variations between individuals. It shows why his will can only be free within the limits of his personality, what is meant by his spirituality, and why man must begin to assume responsibility for his own restraint.

VII

THE ANATOMIC COUNTERPART OF THE EGO STRUCTURE

We have seen that Rank's conception of the will began from a consideration of the dualism he found expressed in the earliest stage of postnatal
development, so that in adult life the will had two components; his genetic
psychology relates man to the "object" from birth to maturity and is really
a history of his ontogenetic development. Clinically, however, the will appears as a single force whose phases are manifested as "good will" or "bad
will." This may be the reason for the fact that the anatomic site of origin
of the motivating force for his actions has been so elusive; once this dual
origin is understood and the forces allocated to the two main thalamic nuclei,
it is possible to orient the others about them, maintaining their relative position in space and using only the connections previously worked out by the
anatomists. The diencephalon is centrally located beneath the corpus callosum and very difficult to approach without trauma. Pressure on its upper
portion causes instant loss of consciousness and deep coma. Animal investi-
gation obviously cannot give us much information about the human psyche.
Under these circumstances it seems warranted to give serious consideration
to the parallel which has been found and whose further elaboration is now
proposed.

The clue which led to the idea that the ego structure might find an
anatomic counterpart was found in Dr. W. R. Ingram's diagram of hypothalamic connections,[1] shown in Figure 4. Here are seen two nuclei, the
anterior ventral and the median dorsal, located in a structure associated with
feeling, the thalamus, and each with connections to and from the cortex.
The anterior ventral receives an afferent connection from the mammillary
body in the hypothalamus; the medial dorsal gives off a connection to the
median portion of the hypothalamus. The thalamus, with its cortical and
hypothalamic connections, thus has such a striking similarity to the realm
of feeling in the ego structure, with its two projection fields in consciousness
and its connections with the instinctive id, that a further study seemed warranted.

[1] Ernst Gellhorn, *Autonomic Regulations: Their Significance for Physiology,
Psychology and Neuropsychiatry* (New York: Interscience Publishers, Inc., 1943).

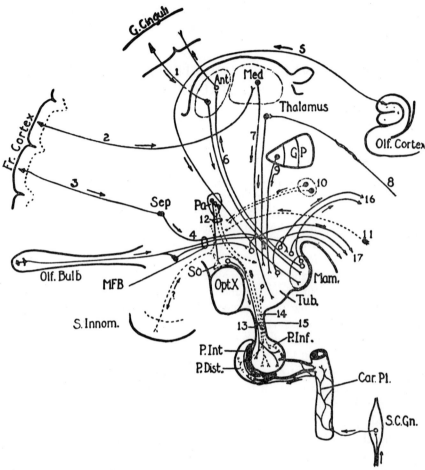

Courtesy of Dr. W. R. Ingram, State University of Iowa

Fig. 4.—Shows Dr. W. R. Ingram's diagram of hypothalamic connections which provided the clue that connected the ego structure with its anatomic counterpart. It shows two thalamic nuclei each with cortical connections and hypothalamic connections which are for the most part those worked out for Rank's ego structure.

The Thalamus, or Realm of Feeling

Introduction of the will into the motor-sensory system.—It has been indicated that the conscious will and opposing will find an anatomic counterpart in the anterior ventral and dorsomedian nucleus of the thalamus. In Figure 2-A the arrows indicate that each may attempt to influence or even to overpower the other. Therefore it has been a matter of the greatest importance in the further development of this anatomic counterpart to see if intrathalamic connections existed to substantiate the idea that the AV and DM nuclei might influence each other.

The gray matter of the thalamus is separated into its medial and lateral parts by the internal medullary lamina which penetrates into it from the *stratum zonale* and bifurcates at its anterior end to enclose partly its rostral pole. This internal medullary lamina is formed by myelinated fibers, which partly form the connections between some of the nuclei. Many of these connections are given[2] and, generally speaking, are found between the medial, posterior, and lateral parts, though the descriptions leave some doubt as to the direction of flow; it is here assumed to be mostly from the medial to the lateral mass. But those connections most desired—i.e., those between the anterior ventral nucleus and the ventral and posterior groups of nuclei—are not given. Furthermore the ventralis anterior and the centromedian are said to be association nuclei, but neither of them is given fiber connections to indicate with which nuclei they associate. Under these circumstances the present writer has assumed that association may occur from the anterior ventral by way of the ventralis anterior to the ventral and posterior groups by a process of *diffusion* through the gray matter in which the nuclei lie, a process analagous to that found in other parts of the nervous system and its effectors.

We have seen above that the anterior pole, which includes the anterior ventral nuclei, is partly enclosed by a bifurcation of the internal medullary lamina; this is the nucleus for which connections are sought with the ventral and posterior groups of nuclei. But its enclosure is incomplete on its inferior aspect, where it lies close to the ventralis anterior. The latter, an "association" nucleus, is the most anterior of the ventral group and is here considered to be the connecting link between the anterior ventral nucleus and the lateral mass, so that the conscious will may *diffuse* through the gray matter to the ventral and posterior groups of nuclei as far as the pulvinar.

The dorsomedial nucleus has a rich connection with the lateralis dorsalis lying on its superior lateral surface, as well as with the lateralis posterior lying behind it; the lateralis dorsalis in turn has connections with the ventral group and with the lateralis posterior, which continues posteriorly as the pulvinar. Through the lateralis dorsalis the dorsomedial thus has connections with the lateral mass so that the opposing will, like the conscious will, has access to the ventral group as far posteriorly as the pulvinar. But it is this ventral and posterior group which connects with the cerebral cortex, the ventrolateral to the motor cortex, the ventroposterolateral to the post-

---

[2] See John F. Fulton, *Physiology of the Nervous System* (New York: Oxford University Press, 1949), pp. 273–75.

The main thalamic nuclei are separated and represented diagrammatically to show their approximate relation to each other and their connections. The dorsomedial connects with the ventral group and with the posterior group through the lateralis dorsalis; it receives connections from the posterior group through the lateralis posterior. The ventralis anterior associates the anterior ventral with the ventral and posterior groups by "diffusion".

The cortical areas to which the ventral and posterior groups project are shown in Walker's diagram in Fig 6.

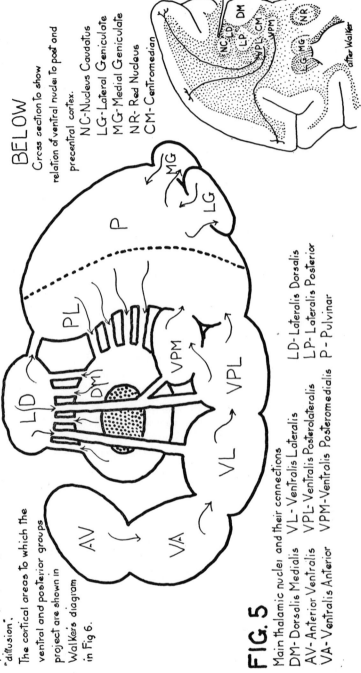

BELOW

Cross section to show relation of ventral nuclei to post and precentral cortex.

NC- Nucleus Caudatus
LG- Lateral Geniculate
MG- Medial Geniculate
NR- Red Nucleus
CM- Centromedian

after Walker

FIG. 5

Main thalamic nuclei and their connections

DM- Dorsalis Medialis   VL- Ventralis Lateralis   LD- Lateralis Dorsalis
AV- Anterior Ventralis   VPL- Ventralis Posterolateralis   LP- Lateralis Posterior
VA- Ventralis Anterior   VPM- Ventralis Posteromedialis   P- Pulvinar

central gyrus, the ventroposteromedial to the face area, the posterolateral to the parietal lobe (exclusive of the postcentral gyrus), and the pulvinar to Area 19, immediately adjacent to the visual cortex and including the posterior sylvian receptive region adjacent to the auditory projection area. These connections, shown in Figure 5, permit access of both the conscious will and the opposing will *together* to all the portions of the cortex mentioned above. The action of the lateralis dorsalis must then be to co-ordinate the cortical activity of the motor, sensory, and associative areas connected by to-and-fro connections with the ventrolateral, ventroposterolateral, ventroposteromedial, and posterolateral nuclei. Walker's diagram showing the cortical areas that represent these thalamic nuclei is presented in Figure 6.

If the principle of diffusion of the energy of the conscious will through the gray matter of the lateral mass of the thalamus as far posterior as the pulvinar holds good, and it seems possible that it does, then the connections to this mass from the dorsomedial nucleus via the lateralis dorsalis would unite the energy of the opposing will with that of the conscious will to form what we know clinically as the human will, and this could be distributed to the cortex as follows:

1. The will force would pass to the motor cortex by the well-known connections between the VL nucleus and Areas 4 and 6, the motor area being supplied by the conscious will or AV nucleus with a slight scattering of fibers to the premotor area, and the premotor area by the opposing will or DM nucleus with a scattering of fibers to the motor area. The hitherto unexplained interruption in this nucleus between the proprioceptive data from the cerebellum via the brachium conjunctivum and red nucleus, and the fibers to the motor cortex, would make possible the introduction of the will at this point. This would be particularly important when such activities as walking and talking were being learned. But when these activities became established and automatic responses to the will, they would be governed by the character gradually established in the prefrontal lobe (see later discussion).

2. The will force would pass to the postcentral gyrus by the connections between the VPL nucleus and this sensory area, the opposing will or DM nucleus supplying the majority of the fibers and the conscious will or AV nucleus the minority, for points evoking motor response are found in this area. The fibers carrying sensory data from the lemnisci are interrupted in this nucleus, and the introduction of the will at this point would provide the will with necessary information and project this to the cortex for suitable cortical activity.

3. The will force would pass to the motor and sensory face area of the cortex from the VPM nucleus, which receives sensory data from the trigeminal nucleus (and tractus solitarius?) and in which the motor activity

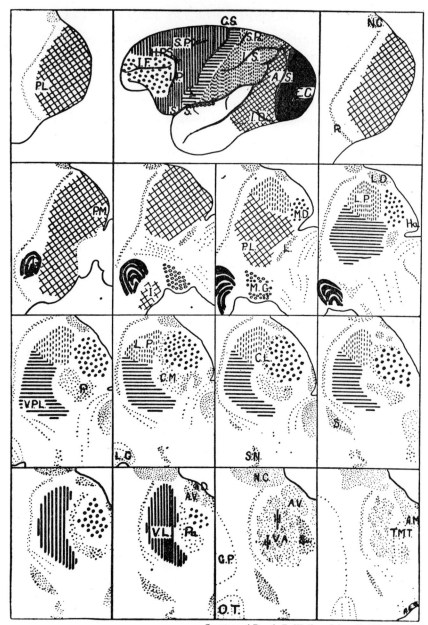

FIG. 6.—Walker's Diagram of thalamocortical projections to show cortical areas representing thalamic nuclei (Walker, *J. Nerv. Ment. Dis.*, LXXXV [1937], 254).

AD N. anterodorsalis	IF Sulcus frontalis inferior	SN Substantia nigra
AM N. anteromedialis		SP Sulcus precentralis superior
AS Sulcus parieto-occipitalis	IO Sulcus occipitalis inferior	SPo Sulcus postcentralis superior
CL N. centralis lateralis	IP Sulcus precentralis inferior (lower limb)	SS Sulcus sylvii
CS Sulcus centralis	IS Sulcus intraparietalis	Su N. Submedius
EC Fissura calcarina externa	OT Tractus opticus	TMT Tractus mammillo-thalamicus
HPS Sulcus precentralis inferior (upper limb)	P N. parafascicularis	VA N. ventralis anterior
	Pa N. paracentralis	

of the fifth, seventh, ninth, tenth (eleventh?), and twelfth cranial nerves originates.

4. The will force would pass from the PL nucleus to the associative area—i.e., to the parietal lobe, exclusive of the postcentral gyrus—where the motor and sensory impulses would be co-ordinated.

5. Lastly, the will force would pass to the pulvinar, which has to-and-fro connections with Area 19 and is postulated here to receive data from the eyes and ears through diffusion from the external and medial geniculate bodies.

Significance of dual control of the motor cortex.—This conception provides a dual control for the motor cortex, so long suspected by physiologists, and affords an explanation for the expression through the cortex of development of personality from its earliest beginnings after birth to its phasic manifestations in adult life. This expression through the cortex portrays the personality characteristics in attitude (posture), facial expression, speech, and action. For example, dejection or elation may be expressed by attitude and facial expression alone, speech being merely a more elaborate and detailed expression, and action a more final one. But before proceeding further with the elaboration of these methods of cortical expression, it will be necessary to explain how this dual control operates through the VPM nucleus of the thalamus to control the motor and sensory cortex of the face area and its pyramidal and extrapyramidal projections to the brain stem nuclei concerned with the facial mechanism. For this facial mechanism is the most vivid of these methods of expression.

The facial mechanism.—The VPM, or arcuate nucleus, not only subserves the "facial mechanism, including mouth, tongue, larynx, etc." but "receives the principal projections from the trigeminal nuclei and sends projections to the sensory face area of the cerebral cortex."[3] The facial mechanism thus involves the activity of the fifth, seventh, ninth, tenth (eleventh?), and twelfth cranial nerves. The nuclei of these nerves receive pyramidal projections (in the adult) from the face area of the precentral gyrus, Area 4, by way of the corticopontine tract; but they also receive extrapyramidal projections from the premotor area (Area 6). The principal path for these extrapyramidal projections is the ansa lenticularis. It terminates *inter alia* in the motor nuclei of the fifth, in the facial nuclei, the ambiguous nuclei, and the hypoglossal nuclei.[4] These are in the group just mentioned as receiving projections from Area 4 by way of the pyramidal tract, and it may therefore be assumed that *extrapyramidal* as well as *pyramidal* projections reach the nuclei of the fifth, seventh, ninth, tenth, and twelfth cranial

[3] Fulton, *op. cit.*, p. 271.
[4] *Ibid.*, p. 488.

nerves. These are called special visceral efferent nerves and lie in a ventro-lateral column in the tegmentum.[5]

The sensory function of the VPM nucleus is mediated through the sensory portion of the trigeminal nerve and by a visceral afferent column in the tegmentum, the tractus solitarius, in which end the visceral afferent fibers of the facial, glossopharyngeal, and vagus nerves. The nuclei of the trigeminal, and presumably of the tractus solitarius, send fibers to the VPM nucleus, which in turn finds cortical representation in the lateral portion of Area 3-1.

Experimental evidence is found to connect the premotor cortex, Area 6, with the facial mechanism. For suitable stimulation of Area 6a alpha under local anesthesia in the human causes "individual movements of the face, mandible and tongue" and similar stimulation of Area 6b alpha causes sustained, rhythmic co-ordinated movements of lips, tongue, mandibles, pharynx, and larynx, i.e., chewing, licking, swallowing, mastication, and outspoken vocalization.[6] From these cortical areas arise the extrapyramidal projections, whereas the pyramidal projections arise from the face area of the precentral gyrus, Area 4. Dual control of the facial mechanism is thus on a firm structural basis in the anatomic counterpart of the ego structure.

Earliest expressions of personality.—The nuclei connected with the facial mechanism are involved *inter alia* in the first cry after birth and in nursing activity, which the present writer conceives to be the earliest expressions of the ego. For the cry is a cry of protest by the opposing will (DM nucleus) against the first onrush of stimuli from the outer world, and nursing activity is an expression of the primitive will with its content of libido (medial mammillary nucleus). But during this early stage of existence the pyramidal tract has been shown to be undeveloped and it seems likely therefore that the primitive will at first activates only the fibers that pass from the VPM nucleus to Area 6.

Later expressions of the personality.—As the infant develops further in response to the mother's love (positive identification) and has more human characteristics and more conscious purpose, or will, and as Area 4 and the pyramidal tract develop, control of these nuclei would pass as well to the pyramidal tract. And later on in adult life dual control of the VPM nucleus and facial mechanism would give full play to elation or dejection and to the various delicate nuances of facial expression of personality. Speech, as a more elaborate method of expression, is mediated through the same cortical area and presumably through the VPM nucleus but, as a learned procedure, seems to have a special center in the pars parvicellularis of the DM nucleus,

[5] Stephen W. Ranson, *The Anatomy of the Nervous System* (rev. by Sam L. Clark; Philadelphia and London: W. B. Saunders Company, 1947), p. 207.
[6] Fulton, *op. cit.*, p. 424.

i.e., in the character. The VPM nucleus through its dual cortical control of most of the cranial nerves thus gives outlet to the personality by facial expression and speech.

But the primitive will finds expression through the VL nucleus (soma) as well as through the VPM nucleus and cranial nerves. Here we find that general motor activity is at first spasmodic, involves proximal muscle groups (Area 6) and is without apparent purpose. However, as the months go by these movements, like those of the special visceral efferent group, gradually come under conscious control of the will. That is to say, more developing fibers project to Area 4 and so become corticospinal or pyramidal.

Personality expression through attitude and action.—In adult life dual control of the somatic musculature is afforded by the VL nucleus, Area 4, and the pyramidal tract on the one hand, and the VL nucleus, Area 6, and the extra pyramidal fibers on the other. The projections from Area 6 pass by way of the basal ganglia, ansa lenticularis, and red nucleus, and by the corticorubral tract and red nucleus to the rubrospinal tract.[7] Since the extrapyramidal fibers serve muscles particularly concerned with automatic maintenance of posture, and the pyramidal fibers serve muscles more concerned with purposeful and often finer movements, hardening of the will from increased sadismus would become evident in postural attitude as well as in facial expression. Action as the last result of this hardening may become final and irrevocable, if aggressive enough, and so effect the lives of other persons. Many crimes of violence result from this hardening of the will, which process completely overcomes the feeling content of the conscious will.

The conception that the primitive will is first expressed through Area 6 and the extrapyramidal system, and that the conscious will is expressed through Area 4 and the pyramidal system as it develops, seems to the present writer of the greatest significance for clinical understanding of the psychoneuroses. For if it is understood that the development of the neurotic has been partially arrested at a primitive stage then his movements will be more under the influence of the primitive will and the extrapyramidal system and his behavior more childlike in some respects. One of the most frequent complaints of these persons is of fatigability, which increases as the neurosis continues into middle life. Most occupations require a considerable concentration of the will on whatever is being done and when the conscious will and pyramidal system are, so to speak, underdeveloped the fatigue from concentrated effort becomes understandable. Primitive or childlike postures such as increased lumbar lordosis and dorsal kyphosis, or even scoliosis in response to underdevelopment of the right side of the body, which is connected with expression of the conscious will, might thus be explained as results of impeded personality development.

7 *Ibid.,* p. 488.

The execution of purposeful ideas.—All the motor portion of the frontal cortex, Areas 4 and 6, and the whole of the parietal lobe including the post-central gyrus, Areas 3-1-2, and the association area of the parietal lobe are said to be potentially sensory areas, for stimulating them by applying strychnine gives rise to somatic sensations in related portions of the body. This large potentially sensory area is served by four thalamic nuclei, the VL, VPL, VPM, and LP, all interconnected as shown in Figure 5. The three cortical portions into which it is divided—motor, sensory, and associative—are intimately connected by association fibers and have, as well, to-and-fro connections with the four thalamic nuclei. Animal experimentation and parietal lesions in humans have shown that interruption of these association fibers by lesions of the motor cortex, sensory cortex, or associative area result in lessened ability to combine the use of the muscles and the proprioceptive and somatic impulses consciously and purposefully. The present writer therefore believes that the above areas—this whole complex of motor, sensory, and associative cortex, which is served by four thalamic nuclei all connected eventually with the AV and DM nuclei—subserve the execution of ideas or will purposes which derive from the site of the character in the prefrontal lobe and pass caudally. It would thus be the character as developed from the will and opposing will which uses this cortex for purposeful self-expression.

Relation of the will forces to the outer world.—The lateral and medial geniculate bodies are nuclei of the posterior group, are under cover of and in closs association with the pulvinar, and, like the ventral nuclei, lie in the gray matter of the thalamus. Their general structure resembles that of the VL and VPL nuclei in so far as fibers from the special sense organs to the cortex are interrupted in them. Now if the process of diffusion of the will impulses be applied to the geniculate bodies, as has here been done with the nuclei in the ventral group, a satisfactory explanation would be given for all the will phenomena disclosed by clinical study of the psychotherapeutic relationship: the will would become effective at the interruption of the afferent fibers from the eyes and ears to the geniculate bodies and project the stimuli to the respective areas in the calcarine and auditory cortices; the visual image or sound impulse would then return to the geniculate bodies which give off connections to the pulvinar, and thence to the DM nucleus by way of the connections from the LP nucleus (see Fig. 5). The opposing will would thus be directly receptive to visual and auditory stimuli from the outer world by way of return connections from these cortical areas via the geniculate bodies to the posterior thalamic nuclei. It would then be possible for the individual to identify positively or negatively with the outer world as he does with the mother.

Relation of the character to the outer world.—This identification with the outer world forms an important part of our character which, as a product of interaction of the will and opposing will, is here presumed to be located in the prefrontal lobe, Areas 9, 10, 11, and 12. As indicated in the preceding paragraphs a possible direct path has been found between the DM nucleus and the outer world via the geniculate bodies. There are also direct paths which might serve to connect the *character* and the outer world. For the superior longitudinal fasciculus, the superior occipitofrontal fasciculus and the inferior occipitofrontal fasciculus might conduct impulses from the occipital lobe and the auditory receptive area, to the prefrontal lobe.

The character expresses itself through impulses passing cephalad from Areas 9, 10, 11, and 12 toward the parastriate and striate areas; the superior longitudinal fasciculus affords a path for impulses passing rostrally from these areas toward the character in the prefrontal lobe. It seems probable, then, that these two streams meet in the various cortical areas so that the performance of any definite task may be carried out under the guidance of the constantly changing order of the data from the outer world. The performance of this task would thus involve the cortex, but the real motor power would come from the thalamus, where the will and its feeling component on the one hand meet the opposing will and its content of outer world data on the other.[8]

The dual path by which these data reach the DM nucleus—one transcortical via Areas 9, 10, 11, and 12, the other subcortical via the geniculate bodies and other posterior thalamic nuclei—would account for all the psychological aberrations, uncontrollable impulses, purposeful mistakes, dreams, and other weird phenomena that distort the lives of so many persons. For the character as built up by identifications with the mother may develop so as to be at cross-purposes with the will forces in the thalamus. The former is, so to speak, behavioristic, the latter truly biologic. When the two are not *en rapport* difficulty ensues.

In this connection a distinction between character and personality emphasized by Rank should be mentioned. Character is the product of the will and opposing will as built up in the prefrontal lobe by identification with the mother and her milieu. It is behavioristic and depends on the milieu to support its beliefs and prejudices. Personality on the other hand is more definitely a product of stronger will forces in the thalamus and is built up with less dependence on the mother and her milieu but in accord with the ethical principles and restraints of its own particular superego.

Recall of images and sounds.—One must suppose that data from the outer world which reach Areas 17, 18, and 19 are not recognized for some time by a newborn child and that the nipple is the first object comprehended. But in

---

[8] It seems very significant to the present writer that James W. Papez, working independently and starting from a purely anatomic standpoint, has arrived at a quite similar conception of thalamocortical function. See *Am. J. of Psychol.*, LVII, July 1944, 291–316.

a few months the mother is recognized; Areas 17 and 18 must therefore have been sensitized to her image and Area 19 to both her image and the sound of her voice. These earliest images and sounds are quite forgotten but those dating from between four and six years may be remembered. Therefore it is here postulated that at this period not only the thalamic nuclei connected with facial expression, speech, and action, and their association (namely the VL, VPL, VPM, and LP) nuclei have assumed active control of the body through the cortex, but also that the visual images and the sounds associated with them in Area 19 pass to the pulvinar, where they are stored as memories. Since the will might have access to this storehouse, as previously described (Fig. 5), memories of years gone by might be recalled or used in a dream. It might be necessary however for this memory to be projected by way of the lateral geniculate body to the visual cortex for organization, or even for images *created anew* by the will to be so projected. Indeed, it is quite possible that the cortex participates in much of the inner activity of the will, for this is often accompanied by silent movements of the lips as in speech; and the fact that after amputation of an extremity the individual may be conscious of sensations and movements which do not actually occur would suggest as much. But the fact that after excision of portions of the motor or sensory cortex, or even of the prefrontal lobe, an experimental animal may soon learn to repeat procedures learned before the excision suggests that the memory connected with the procedure is stored elsewhere than in the cortex, and the pulvinar would satisfy this requirement.

The visual apparatus and denial of the will.—Denial of the will has been shown to play a large part in all our thinking and acting. This is particularly evident in the psychoanalytic concepts where the ego has been subjected to two great forces: (1) the *inner* compulsion of libido, which is "natural" and therefore insurmountable, and (2) the *outer* compulsion of the milieu, which is taken in by identification as a superego. The ego is left almost helpless between them and the effect may be devastating on the individual when the will forces are strong. But introduction of the will and opposing will into the ego structure gives each of these forces some autonomy and makes their product, the personality, more independent of the milieu, with its beliefs and prejudices. The writer believes that this same denial of the will may not only have delayed the discovery of the site of the will in the human brain but also have influenced the interpretation of the visual apparatus. For the eyes develop as an evagination of the diencephalon and, like the face, are a most expressive part of the personality. To the therapist they play a most revealing role by mirroring the fear and dejection or the defiant negativism of the neurotic at his first appointment, his elation when he finds it possible to express his will, his suffering while he is overcoming his denial, his tranquillity when he is about to leave; all these emotions seem to find some expression in the eye. Small wonder then that it has been called the window of the soul. The fact that the optic tracts alone contain more than one-third of the white fibers in the human brain would suggest that they play more than the passive role at present assigned to them in the anatomy and physiology texts. The visual images must not only reach the opposing will (here the DM nucleus) but, like the mother and the milieu, be taken into and become a part of it: the world about us seems actually to be a part of us just as we seem to be a part of it. That is why the relation of the neurotic to the outer world seems to him so tragic as to invite self-destruction—it is a negative one—and why the relation to it of the schizophrenic seems to him unreal: he denies it just as he has identified with and then denied the mother in both a negative and positive sense.

The visual image not only reaches the will forces but is influenced by them. Thus the lover idealizes the image of his mate, the neurotic depreciates, the psychotic falsifies the images of the world he sees about him, the religious fanatic to satisfy his will creates new images where none exist. With all this evidence and the projection mechanism in mind one is inclined to surmise that the visual image is not only projected by the will to the calcarine cortex but taken into the DM nucleus and again projected outward to the retina. The whole process would then run parallel to that by which the infant projects his oral sadismus onto the mother, takes it back by identification as restraint, and again projects it outward, modified, as part of the will. This process can be seen to be a function of the will in the patient-therapist relationship. And efferent fibers in the optic nerve from the lateral geniculate to the retina together with those already suggested here, make it now seem anatomically possible.

Frontal Areas 9, 10, 11, and 12

In Chapter I the character was described as a summation of the experiences by which the biological self struggles to adjust to the social environment. The will psychology, however, showed that this struggle was not actually with the environment but with the opposing will, which became its representative in the ego structure by identifying with it. The character resulting from the adjustment thus became the product of the interaction of the will and opposing will and was shown in Figure 2-D as appended to the opposing will. This structure finds its anatomic counterpart in that part of the frontal lobe, designated as Areas 9, 10, 11, and 12, which is subserved by the pars parvicellularis of the DM nucleus. Of the four parts of this small-celled portion the ventrolateral projects to Area 8, the frontal eye area, the dorsolateral to Areas 45 and 46 (Broca's area), the medial to Area 11, and the central part to Areas 9 and 10.[9] Unlike the motor cortex this portion of

[9] Fulton, *op. cit.*, p. 450.

the frontal lobe does not react to electrical stimulation by motor expression. The reason has now become obvious: this area, active only during consciousness, records the developmental experiences of the will forces and, during waking hours, expresses them as behavior in response to stimuli from the outer world, not in response to electrical stimulation. Much of the experimental work showing autonomic response to electrical stimulation has included Areas 13 and 14, the orbital surface of the frontal lobe, which will be considered under another heading. But some experimentation has shown that distractibility and general intellectual deficit result from *ablation* of these areas. One animal, to cite a particular case, an adolescent affectionate female, had reacted with temper tantrums as the solution of the problems was made increasingly difficult. After removing the prefrontal lobe, but sparing the orbital surface, the animal made much more frequent mistakes in attempting to solve the problems learned before operation but reacted with indifference instead of temper tantrums. Generally the behavior of the frontal-area chimpanzees showed a fatuous equanimity of spirit.[10] Because of the extensive degeneration in the DM nucleus following frontal lobotomy[11] these conclusions are of doubtful significance in relation to Areas 9, 10, 11, and 12. For while these areas are indeed subserved by the pars parvicellularis of the DM nucleus, its *large-celled portion* projects to the orbital surface and in the ego structure represents the opposing will by which "temper tantrums" would be expressed. Therefore one would seriously question whether the degeneration had not also affected the large-celled portion and made it incapable of reacting normally. Or it might have so dulled the receptivity of the small-celled portion as to make it unsusceptible to pain by punishment of the super-ego, which is represented by the orbital surface.

However this may be, there is clinical evidence that Areas 9, 10, 11, and 12 are concerned with the cortical registration of character, which is the product of the will and opposing will, and this is of particular interest because the brain structure was not altered by operation. It shows that, in the case to be cited, the character was modified by treatment and thus that whatever was registered in this portion of the cortex was subject to change.

The case was of a young man who applied for treatment because of stammering. He had been through all the routines usually prescribed for this functional speech aberration without permanent relief and still had a 90 percent impairment. That is to say, his speech was so halting that it took him possibly ten times as long as normal speech would require to make a statement. But he was able to sing or to talk to his dog without showing his impediment. Usually he did better talking to women than to men. His story revealed that he had been completely dominated by his mother and as his

10 Fulton, *op. cit.*, p. 458.
11 *Ibid.*, p. 448.

treatment proceeded it became evident that he had identified negatively with her at the oral stage and that his development had so been partially arrested. His behavior as exemplified by his speech was a compulsive effort to break through the maternal restraints. But there were other characteristics which showed that his will was undeveloped: he feared he would not be able to function properly as a husband (castration complex). He went through the usual reactions and at the termination of the treatment said he felt fully capable of making his own decisions. But his impairment was still at the 90 percent level. At the end of a year he came in for a progress report. This showed that great progress had been made during the interval. He now had perhaps 10 percent impairment and was planning to marry. There was every evidence that his speech had improved along with his will development and it seemed certain that he would completely recover.

The dorsolateral portion of the pars parvicellularis of the DM nucleus is said to project to Broca's area, though these connections have not been completely worked out; the VPM nucleus also projects to Broca's area. Since speech is a learned process it seems likely therefore that the dorso-lateral portion of the pars parvicellularis reaches Broca's area indirectly by way of some portion of the prefrontal cortex and thence transcortically to the speech area. In this way speech might take place either by this trans-cortical path or by way of the VPM nucleus. This would explain the fact that the young man described could have a speech and character deficit as a result of the negative identification with his mother and still be able under certain circumstances to speak normally. In the presence of the mother or of someone whom he could identify with her the transcortical path would be used, when alone with his dog the other. Under normal conditions both of these paths would agree: individual use of the transcortical path in the pres-ence of others would result in stammering, and use of the thalamic path when alone with his dog in normal speech. Sleep speaking could also be explained by this thalamic path.

We have seen that the ventrolateral portion of the pars parvicellularis projects to Area 8 and it seems likely that this projection is also indirect, i.e., to a portion of the prefrontal cortex and thence transcortically to Area 8, where eye movements would also express character.

There remain two portions of the pars parvicellularis: the medial projects to Area 11 and the central to Areas 9 and 10. Possibly these represent the opposing will as modified by the maternal positive and negative identifica-tions. These would then operate from these cortical areas and pass trans-cortically toward the striate area representing the outer world. During sleep, on the other hand, the cortical area would be in abeyance but the will and opposing will might find expression in the dream when suitably provoked.

The fixation of a positive identification in the prefrontal area would explain the domestication of the chimpanzee, "Becky."[12] Under natural conditions she would have been a wild animal but by identifying with her keepers she became gentle and affectionate and eager to co-operate. When the limit of her ability to learn was reached she had conflict between her will and opposing will; the latter protested with temper tantrums and her intellectual ability rapidly diminished. This type of intellectual breakdown is exactly what we find in psychoneurosis. Ideals foreign to the subject have been implanted at an early age by well-meaning parents. Inability to accept and live up to these ideals results in conflict and intellectual deficit. In the case of the young man who stammered, the mother had implanted ideals against which he rebelled. This rebellion was evidenced not only by conflict in his speech but by conflict in other fields. As he began to recover he chose commercial art as a profession which gave him a more individualized method of expression than the more formal profession chosen under the mother's influence. In human beings the whole matter seems to revolve about the question of freedom to select one's own ideal.

But the case of the stammerer also shows that overcoming the impediment is a matter of growth and that this involves changes in the cortex which we must presume lie somewhere in Areas 9, 10, 11, and 12.

Pars Magnocellularis of the DM Nucleus

The large-celled medially placed portion of the DM nucleus, which is the anatomic counterpart of the opposing will, plays perhaps the most significant role in the whole psychic structure for, as demonstrated below, there is reason to believe that it represents the center of parasympathetic activity; some of its connections ascend to the cortex and some descend to the hypothalamus and medulla and it is therefore presumed that the former (the ascending connections) are psychic representatives of the latter (the descending connections). The influence of the pars magnocellularis may be exerted in four directions.

The first path by which the influence of the pars magnocellularis is exerted leads to the orbital surface of the frontal lobe, which is both the anatomic counterpart of the superego and the cortical representative of the vagus nerve,[13] and is for the most part constituted by Areas 13 and 14. That is to say, it activates and is in turn activated by the orbital surface. Here we find the anatomic counterpart for the dreaded superego, which deals out punishment when its authority is denied by the opposing will, from which the voice of man's conscience speaks ex cathedra. Here, in essence, lies the source of his spirituality and of his ethical problem. This is what he attempts to evade

12 Fulton, op. cit., p. 456.
13 Ibid., pp. 273–75.

when he denies his will and rationalizes his libido. The to-and-fro connections between the pars magnocellularis and the orbital surface are those by which the sadomasochistic mechanism would operate. The orbital surface of the neurotic would then be endowed with a specific negativity toward certain methods of expression of the will and certain uses of its accompanying libido since these bring about pain and suffering.

The second path would lead by way of the connections of the DM nucleus shown in Figure 5 to the motor cortex, where it would find expression in action, facial expression, and attitude, but also would lead to the dorso-lateral portion of the pars parvicellularis whence it would be projected trans-cortically to Broca's area for verbal expression. This path would lead to that kind of negativism characterized by the recent statement of a young woman that whatever her mother requested her to do she always wanted to say "no." And this statement was made with such incisiveness, vigor, and determination as to show that the opposing will was indeed expressed in voice, facial expression, and attitude, that it was in fact the largest part of this particular personality.[14]

The third path leads to the hypothalamus which is the anatomic counter-part of the id. This path,[15] which probably reaches the hypothalamus by way of its ventromedial nucleus, permits restraint of the instinctual forces in the id. That is to say, the development of the primitive will and libido, whose site of origin is allocated here to the mammillary body, may be either modi-fied or arrested by the force of the opposing will exerted through these fiber connections. True, the "connections between the anterior nuclei of the hypo-thalamus and the mammillary body though long suspected have not been clearly established."[16] But the path from the DM nucleus to the ventro-medial nucleus which would interrupt these anteropostero connections is so obviously a clinical reality that the present writer feels completely justified in assuming that they exist.

The fourth path leads downward by way of the hypothalamus to the medulla where, when the opposing will is denied, the denial may be justified through the autonomic system by way of general visceral vagus activity. For although we have traced a path (the second) by which the pars magnocellu-laris may reach the VPM nucleus, subserve the "facial mechanism includ-ing the larynx,"[17] project to the precentral motor cortex and thence to the nucleus of the tenth nerve in the medulla to become a *conscious* source of vagus activity (the voice), it also projects to the hypothalamus by the path

[14] See "Verleugnung und Realitätsanpassung," in *Grundzüge einer Genetischen Psychologie*, pp. 150–51.

[15] Fulton, *op. cit.*, p. 273.

[16] *Ibid.*, p. 240.

[17] *Ibid.*, p. 271.

already described whence it may descend to the tegmentum and so down to the general visceral motor nucleus of the vagus where it serves such *unconscious* general visceral function as that of heart and lungs. The pars magnocellularis would thus have both a *conscious* path to the larynx and an *unconscious* path to the viscera.

The Hypothalamus

As description of the anatomic counterpart of the ego structure has proceeded it must have become clear that the instinctual id is here represented by the hypothalamus. Connections have been described between the hypothalamus and the DM nucleus by means of which its pars magnocellularis, or opposing will, could influence the development of the primitive will and libido. One very important part of the hypothalamus, the pituitary, may be briefly discussed at this point because of the possibility that the secretory capacity of its anterior lobe might play a role in determining the strength of what we have called the biological self. In the ego structure we have located the origin of this biological self in the posterior portion of the id and identified it and its appended libido with the mammillary nucleus from which the tractus mammillothalamicus arises and in which the fornix terminates. The two principal anterior nuclei of the hypothalamus, the paraventricular and supraoptic nuclei, are said to be parasympathetic in nature and have quite definite fiber connections with the *posterior* lobe of the pituitary and possibly supply a few fibers to its *anterior* lobe as well. However, it is now believed that the anterior lobe secretions are "humorally regulated either by way of the adrenals or by the direct passage of chemical agents via the portal vessels of the pituitary stalk"[18] whose caliber is controlled by the supraoptic hypophyseal tract. In short, there is "overwhelming evidence"[19] of hypothalamic control of anterior lobe secretion. It would seem probable to the present writer that the paraventricular and supraoptic nuclei are governed from above by the pars magnocellularis of the DM nucleus. Fiber connections which would make this possible are not known but Patrick Wall has disclosed (unpublished) "that unmyelinated projections can be traced from the orbital surface to this anterior group of hypothalamic nuclei and also to the ventromedial group."[20] These connections would place the anterior nuclei and thus the pituitary secretions under the control of what is here taken to be the superego.

The individual with a stronger social self is usually more restrained in his sexual expression, the one with the stronger biological self more inclined

---

[18] Fulton, *op. cit.*, p. 243.
[19] *Loc. cit.*
[20] *Ibid.*, p. 238.

to freer expression. The question arises how much the anterior pituitary contributes to this freer expression. In this connection it must be remembered that libido and sexual potency are not the same, libido being here attributed to the hippocampus and contributing sexual desire and its sublimated derivative feeling to the ego structure, while the anterior pituitary influences the gonads and their development in the somatic sphere. In this sense libido would be primary and the anterior pituitary secondary. And, as will be shown later, the orgasm is a *central* process which is projected to the *periphery* but does not originate there. Women whose pelvic organs have been completely removed may readily achieve the orgasm, and it has been stated that some emasculated men may do the same. Therefore the present writer believes that the anterior pituitary secretion does not determine the predominance of the biological self, indeed, that the psyche is more likely to influence the anterior pituitary secretion.

Since idiopathic epilepsy commonly shows vascular changes in the hippocampus and evidence of marked personality changes it would be a fascinating task to study a group of young epileptics by the Rankian method and attempt to determine what personality elements, if any, enter into this affliction.

The mammillary body.—This is composed of three nuclei, the largest of which is the medial mammillary nucleus. It is the anatomic counterpart of the primitive will, which would thus pass via the mammillothalamic tract to the anterior thalamic group of nuclei. Into it debouch the fornix fibers from the hippocampus.

About the mammillary body has centered a great deal of animal experimentation which proves that it is the site of origin of the so-called "sham rage" reaction in animals. This may be brought about by stimulation of the posterior hypothalamic area and in cats and rats by placement of Horsley-Clark lesions in the ventromedial nucleus of the hypothalamus, also by radical bilateral ablation of the orbital surface.[21] But the orbital surface is in man the anatomic counterpart of the superego, the restraining authority which causes suppression of the opposing will. And a path from the supposed anatomic representative of the opposing will, the pars magnocellularis, leads to the hypothalamus, where we have presumed it terminated in the ventromedian nucleus. If the results of this kind of animal experimentation can be applied to man we find here a path by which suppression of the opposing will by the superego might influence the development of the primitive will and prevent its expression as "rage" (violence).

The hypothalamus, the autonomic system, and psychosomatic disease.—It is noteworthy that during the outbursts of sham rage there are signs of

[21] *Ibid.*, p. 245.

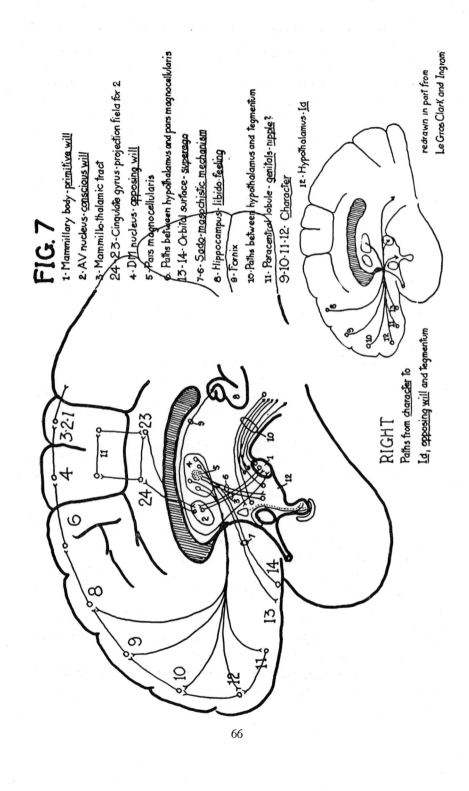

FIG. 7

1 · Mammillary body · primitive will
2 · AV nucleus · conscious will
3 · Mammillo-thalamic tract
24-23 · Cingulate gyrus · projection field for 2
4 · DM nucleus · opposing will
5 · Pars magnocellularis
6 · Paths between hypothalamus and pars magnocellularis
13-14 · Orbital surface · superego
7-6 · Sado-masochistic mechanism
8 · Hippocampus · libido · feeling
9 · Fornix
10 · Paths between hypothalamus and tegmentum
11 · Paracentral lobule · genitals · nipple?
9-10-11-12 · Character
12 · Hypothalamus · Id

RIGHT

Paths from character to
Id, opposing will and tegmentum

redrawn in part from
Le Gros Clark and Ingram

66

strong generalized sympathetic activity. The pupils dilate, the hair stands on end, the heart rate increases, the blood pressure rises, salivation occurs.[22] In suitably prepared animals bouts of extrasystolic arrhythmia can be traced back to the posterior hypothalamic area and they cease when this area is excluded.[23] The site of origin of the sympathetic energy thus seems to be the posterior and lateral hypothalamic areas where nuclei by these names exist; it descends by way of the periventricular system which arises in these areas and passes on down to the spinal cord with many secondary relay systems in the tegmentum and medulla.[24] The mammillary nucleus and the posterior and lateral hypothalamic nuclei thus seem to act as a unit. The former would discharge will energy toward the thalamus, the latter sympathetic energy toward the brain stem and cord.

On the other hand much evidence exists to show that the tuber and anterior hypothalamic nuclei are parasympathetic in nature.[25] The path by which this parasympathetic energy could descend to the medulla is not known and we can only speculate as to what course it might take. But there is an ascending path for the vagus afferents to the mammillary body by way of the mammillary peduncle,[26] which arises in the ventral tegmental nucleus and this might send fibers to the DM nucleus by way of the medial hypothalamic nuclei.[27] And we have traced a path from the DM nucleus to the hypothalamus. The descending parasympathetic energy might therefore descend to the medulla by way of one of the diffuse descending paths accompanying the periventricular system to the medulla.[28] The vagus nucleus in the medulla would thus be related to the DM nucleus by to-and-fro paths through the hypothalamus.

The pars magnocellularis of the DM nucleus which represents the opposing will would then be the site of origin of the parasympathetic, and the posterior and lateral hypothalamic nuclei, which are activated with the mammillary body representing the primitive will, the site of origin of sympathetic energy. And the descending connections given above would explain the downward projection of the will to the soma previously mentioned, and bring the various psychosomatic diseases into direct relation with psychic activity on the hypothalamic or unconscious level in the id. Most of the connections discussed in the text are shown in Figure 7.

But it is characteristic of much psychosomatic disease that the patient is not troubled by obvious emotional disturbance or by will phenomena; on the contrary he is often a person of considerable ability and determination, and in no sense neurotic. If we consider his disease to result from an imbalance

---

[22] Fulton, *op. cit.*, p. 244.   [23] *Ibid.*, p. 246.   [24] *Ibid.*, p. 241.
[25] *Ibid.*, p. 246.   [26] *Ibid.*, p. 240.   [27] *Ibid.*, p. 241.
[28] *Loc. cit.*

between the sympathetic and parasympathetic portions of the nervous system, then the connections described by Patrick Wall (see above) from the orbital surface to the supraoptic and ventromedial nuclei, or, more probably, those described by Ward and McColloch[29] from the orbital surface to the nucleus paraventricularis (parasympathetic) and to the posterior hypothalamic area (sympathetic) might cause this imbalance through suppression exerted by the superego to one or the other of these sites.[30]

In the preceding paragraph reasons have been given to postulate that the parasympathetic arises in the DM nucleus and the sympathetic in the mammillary body. And these two structures have been here understood to be the sites of origin respectively of the opposing will and of the primitive will. Furthermore, incontrovertible evidence has been found of sympathetic and parasympathetic activity through the cortex.[31] The present writer therefore concludes first that what he has called the primitive will is in reality a psychic representative of the sympathetic, and second that the opposing will is a corresponding representative of the parasympathetic. He has shown that in the thalamus connections exist which make possible the union of both of these forces into what is known clinically as the will: energy from each of the above sources is poured, so to speak, into the pool of gray matter constituted by the lateral and posterior masses of the thalamus; in this pool lie the nuclei concerned with reception of data from the outer and inner worlds as well as the nuclei concerned with activity of the soma in space and time; connected with each of the main sources of this energy in the thalamus is a cortical area which permits its projection in the form of an idea, positive in the case of the sympathetic and negative in the case of the parasympathetic; these positive and negative ideas represent the phasic changes in the nature of the will.

The idea of this pool of energy brings into being a new conception of physiologic energy, an energy which represents not the activity manifested in speech or active movement, but something more like a source of supply, something manifested in consciousness and in apperception of events and conditions of the outer world. This pool would be gradually exhausted by the expenditure of its energy in thought and action until sleep became imperative; this then would re-establish the supply until on awakening consciousness would soon be fully active and the self and outer world again be fully apperceived. This idea of a pool of energy, of a source of supply, which would gradually be depleted by activity and replenished by sleep is quite unique, has no exact counterpart in the nervous system, though there is some evidence

[29] *J. Neurophysiol.*, X (1947), 309–14.
[30] Fulton, *op. cit.*, p. 452.
[31] Fulton, *op. cit.*, p. 468.

of similar activity in a peripheral resting nerve which when supplied with nitrogen instead of oxygen continues to form heat though at a diminishing rate indicative of gradual depletion of its reserve of energy.[32]

It may be noted that the conception of a pool of psychic energy in the thalamus as the main seat of consciousness of the self presents a situation analagous to that existing a century ago in regard to the conduction of an impulse along a peripheral nerve. Muller asserted then that the time required for transmission of a sensation from the periphery to the brain and the return reflex movements of the muscles was infinitely small and unmeasurable, in other words, that the energy involved was psychic and imponderable. Similarly the elements that enter into consciousness of self have heretofore been presumed psychic and imponderable. But only six years after Muller's statement Helmholtz proved that the nerve impulse was finite and now Rank, too, seems to have hit upon will principles that are finite and find representation in the brain structure.[33]

The hypothalamus and the respiratory center.—A relation between the respiratory center and psychic activity is frequently observed by the therapist on both the negative and positive sides. The neurotic often heaves a deep sigh when in a depressed mood, i.e., when he is denying his opposing will. Or his breathing may accelerate when he feels guilty about saying what he does, i.e., when he says it fearfully in spite of his superego. Both the sigh and the accelerated breathing are connected with activity of his opposing will. On the other hand his breathing may deepen somewhat with the upsurge of feeling connected with full acceptance of his conscious will. Sobbing and laughter which are due to spasmodic action of the diaphragm are negative and positive expressions respectively of the opposing will and the conscious will. For the former is an expression of pain inflicted masochistically either by the self or, through identification, by another, while the latter is usually at some one else's expense and so slightly sadistic.

A somewhat similar relation is observed by the experimenter, for stimulation of the orbital surface results in arrest of respiration, and it is therefore said to play an important part in regulating breathing. Indeed, small unmyelinated projections have been traced from the orbital surface of the frontal lobe directly to the anterior group of hypothalamic nuclei and also to the ventromedial group.[34] And connections must exist between the orbital surface and the posterior hypothalamic area because the latter is activated by strychninization of the posterior orbital gyri.[35] There is thus ample anatomic

[32] John F. Fulton, ed., *A Textbook of Physiology* (by William H. Howell; Philadelphia and London: W. B. Saunders Company, 1949), p. 54.

[33] *Ibid*, p. 9.

[34] Fulton, *Phys. N.S.*, p. 238.

[35] *Ibid.*, p. 450.

justification for assuming that the forms of psychic activity observed by the therapist may influence the respiratory center by way of hypothalamic-medullary connections, i.e., unconsciously at the level of the id.

Now the respiratory center lies in the reticular formation of the medulla just over the inferior olive and consists of an inspiratory and a more dorsally placed expiratory portion. These portions are so connected that activity in one inhibits activity in the other. Impulses from the two centers are conducted over descending spinal pathways and stimulate the final motoneurones which innervate the respiratory muscles.[36] Inflation stimulates receptors in the lungs which activate the expiratory center by way of the vagus nerve; this inhibits the inspiratory center and allows expiration to proceed. Deflation deactivates the expiratory center through other receptors in the lungs and the inspiratory center again discharges impulses. The rhythmic activity of respiration thus depends on these vagus afferents.

A somewhat similar inhibitory mechanism called the pneumotaxic center lies in the tegmentum in the upper few millimeters of the pons. Ordinarily it is subsidiary to the vagal reflex mechanism but may substitute for it if the vagus be cut. In the intact animal when the heat loss mechanism in the hypothalamus is stimulated and panting results, impulses from the heat loss regulating centers in the hypothalamus dominate the respiratory rhythm.

The present writer believes it likely that the activity of the respiratory center is not only governed negatively by the DM nucleus but positively by the posterior hypothalamic area which is so closely associated with activity of the mammillary nucleus that the two act as a unit. For here, in one of the nuclei from which the sympathetic arises, is found a matrix of small cells all motor in function.[37] The impulses from these cells would descend by the periventricular system to the medulla to activate the inspiratory portion of the respiratory center. This would explain the acceleration and deepening of respiration with positive expression of the primitive will at the unconscious level in the id, for it would activate the posterior hypothalamic nucleus. This circuit of positive motor impulses from the posterior hypothalamic area to the inspiratory center and of negative inhibitory vagus impulses from the hypothalamus to the expiratory center and back to the hypothalamus would take in the pneumotaxic center; this and the respiratory center itself would be subsidiary to the hypothalamus but capable of independent action under the conditions given above.

The hypothalamus and hysterical hyperpnea.—In hysteria the negative identification with the mother is very strong, the positive projections onto the mother if not entirely withdrawn remain primitive, the opposing will is turned into the ego structure and restrains the development of the primitive

[36] Fulton, *Textbk. Phys.*, p. 837.
[37] Fulton, *Phys. N.S.*, p. 238.

will through the id. The resulting immature individual is inadequate to meet the struggle life demands. A difficult situation therefore arouses fear. This may be projected onto the object but its cause lies in the domination of the ego by the opposing will and suppression of this by the superego. Translated into anatomic terms this would mean that the pars magnocellularis of the DM nucleus had turned into the diencephalon at an early age to arrest the development of the mammillary nucleus and that it thereafter remained the dominant factor. This domination could easily affect the respiratory center through the connections given above and bring about an exaggerated activity of the expiratory center. This would be met in turn by overactivity of the inspiratory center and result in hyperpnea. Such activity is actually seen in hysterical attacks and may continue until tetany results from alkalinization of the blood. In the view of the present writer this hyperpnea is not conscious activity any more than the denial of the mother from which the hysteria arose is conscious. The latter is the result of arrested psychological development and the hyperpnea a fear reaction which would be brought on by physiological means at the unconscious level of the hypothalamus.

The hypothalamus and the sleep function.—The hypothetical control of respiration by the posterior hypothalamic area and the DM nucleus—the former supplying the continual drive toward life through the mammillary nucleus, the latter regulating, modifying, and contributing rhythmicity—finds a parallel in the somewhat similar periodicity of the day and night phases of waking and sleeping. Consideration of the DM nucleus, or opposing will, as a center which is irritable both to incoming sensory stimuli from the outer world and to stimuli from the mammillary nucleus, or primitive will, would seem to the present writer to explain satisfactorily the sleep function. For when the primitive will center failed to function fully, either through fatigue or relaxation (habit), the DM nucleus would be less irritated and so able to ignore incoming sensory stimuli. Or when the DM nucleus was so fatigued from incoming stimuli that it was incapable of continuing to receive them they would be ignored. Since consciousness is connected with activity of the DM nucleus sleep would result in either case, and the hypothalamus would then take over on the unconscious level of the id. Sleep would thus be a phase of psychic function which depended on the relative activity of the same centers which determined the activity of the respiratory center.[38]

In a still broader sense the relative activity of the DM nucleus and the posterior hypothalamic area with its mammillary nucleus would determine the eventual fate of the individual just as we have postulated that they may control his immediate respiratory activity. For when the biological self is so strong that it overpowers the social self and exceeds all restraint, the indi-

[38] See the stimulating and similar ideas of E. Tromner, "Schlaffunktion und Schlaforgan," *Deutsche Zeitschrift für Nervenheilkunde*, CIV–CV (1928), 191–203.

vidual inevitably follows a path that leads to destruction just as the inspiratory center when freed from control by the vagus and by the pneumotaxic center leads to asphyxiation in maintained inspiration.

The conscious will and the respiratory center.—In the preceding discussion of psychic regulation of the respiratory center consideration has been given only to unconscious control through the hypothalamus, the anatomic counterpart of the id. But the same regulatory elements operate on the conscious level through the thalamus and cortex. That is to say, both inspiration and expiration may be consciously controlled by the will. Furthermore, breathing may be consciously arrested for some minutes by the opposing will until the primitive will finally breaks through this restraint and compels inspiration: the will is stronger than the opposing will. This conscious control might operate from the AV and DM nuclei via the VPM nuclei (see Fig. 5) to the face area of the motor cortex and thence to the respiratory center, where the impulses would be distributed to the final motoneurones in the cervical and upper dorsal spinal cord. For the spinal accessory nerve is subserved by the VPM nucleus, whose impulses reach their final motoneurones in the first six cervical segments and the diaphragm finds its source of supply in the third, fourth, and fifth.

A similar distribution of the will and opposing will might occur in speaking or playing a wind instrument. But these are *learned* activities and would therefore find their starting point in the dorsolateral portion of the pars parvicellularis, where the thalamic center for speech is found. In this connection it is interesting that weak stimulation of Area 6b beta causes slowing of respiration[39] and that this area adjoins Broca's area through which this speech center operates. It might therefore be similarly controlled by the pars parvicellularis.

The Cornu Ammonis (Hippocampus) as a Source of Libido

"Libido" is used here in the sense in which Rank used it. He states in the Foreword of his *Grundzüge einer Genetischen Psychologie* : "In that book [his *Trauma of Birth*] libido development was traced in one direction back to its ontogenetic origin in the intra-uterine situation, and followed in the other direction by means of its transformation into feeling and understanding through our culture and growth up to the very point of psychoanalytic perception itself." In other words libido is the desire to return to the mother and derives from the original union with the mother in the womb.

Ammon's horn is an effector organ whose main path of discharge is the fornix. This enters the medial mammillary nucleus which we have designated as the anatomic counterpart of the primitive will. The idea so long current that Ammon's horn was an essential part of the rhinencephalon has

[39] Fulton, *Phys. N.S.*, p. 424.

been completely refuted experimentally; it is also contradicted by the fact that the size and development of Ammon's horn are in inverse proportion to the importance of the sense of smell in the phylogenetic ascent of mammals. For Ammon's horn, together with the medial mammillary nucleus, the mammillothalamic tract, the anterior ventral nucleus of the thalamus, and the cingular gyrus reach the peak of their development in man. If comparisons are made between the size of the olfactory bulb and Ammon's horn in various mammals, man has relatively (and absolutely) the largest.[40] For these reasons and because of the suggestion of Papez[41] that the hippocampus, the medial mammillary nucleus, the mammillothalamic tract, the anterior ventral nucleus of the thalamus, the cingular gyrus, and their interconnections constitute a harmonious mechanism for the elaboration of central emotion, Ammon's horn has been studied with the idea in mind that it might be the site of origin of libido.

Eroticism and the orgasm as central processes.—It has already been stated that libido must originate at the very core of the central nervous system. This idea seem to the present writer to be completely substantiated by a case of epileptiform focal seizures reported by Erickson[42] and summarized by Fulton[43] as follows:

A serious-minded housewife of normal behavior began at the age of forty-three to experience spells of intense erotic sensations referred to the left side of her vagina—as though she were having sexual intercourse and orgasms on one side only. Over a period of ten years the symptoms increased in frequency and severity and, until the patient developed a left hemiparesis, the diagnosis of nymphomania had been foisted on her. On surgical exploration a small vascular tumor was disclosed on the medial surface of the hemisphere impinging on the motor and sensory representation of the genitalia.

The cortical motor and sensory representation of the genitals, and possibly of the nipple too,[44] is in the paracentral lobule which lies on the medial surface of the hemisphere directly above the cingular gyrus. The anterior ventral nucleus of the thalamus, or the conscious will, projects to this lobule as well as to the cingular gyrus and this projection would provide the fateful connection between the libidinous will and the sexual organs and make auto-eroticism understandable anatomically. Representation of the nipple in the paracentral lobule would strongly support Rank's conception that the first

[40] Alf Brodal, "The Hippocampus and the Sense of Smell," *Brain*, LXX (1947), 208. Brodal's excellent review should be studied by those interested in the hippocampus.

[41] J. W. Papez, "A Proposed Mechanism of Emotion," *Arch. of Neurol. and Psych.*, XXXV (1937), 725.

[42] T. C. Erickson, "Erotomania (Nymphomania) as an Expression of Cortical Epileptiform Discharge," *Arch. of Neurol. and Psych.*, LIII (1945), 226–31.

[43] *Phys. N.S.*, p. 399.

[44] W. Penfield and Th. Rasmussen, *The Cerebral Cortex of Man* (New York: The Macmillan Company, 1950), p. 45.

object relationship (mouth-nipple) is libidinous in nature. On the other hand, the perineal sphincters would be under the control of the opposing will or dorsomedial nucleus, for the "sphincter ego" is the first beginning of the superego. Defiance of the mother's injunction to cleanliness would thus represent unrestrained activity of the opposing will and acceptance of toilet training its control by the superego.

The conscious will represents impulses from the primitive will center (the mammillary nucleus), modified by the opposing will (the dorsomedial nucleus) ; it would project whatever content it might have to the cingular gyrus where that content would become conscious as an idea. The cingular gyrus, like the paracentral lobule, has an anterior agranular portion, Area 24, and a posterior granular portion, Area 23.

While the AV nucleus projects to Area 24, it is reported that only Area 23 projects back to the AV nucleus.[45] The genital area thus lies directly above Area 24, the supposed projection field of the will, and both are supplied by the AV nucleus (the will).

But equally important for understanding of this case of so-called nymphomania are connections from the cingular gyrus via the cingulum to Ammon's horn. For they complete a circuit from Ammon's horn, the supposed source of libido, via the fornix, mammillary body, mammillothalamic tract, and AV nucleus to the paracentral lobule, and thence back via Area 23 and fibers which pass by way of the cingulum to Ammon's horn (see Fig. 8). The vascular tumor disclosed at operation evidently stimulated the paracentral lobule strongly and this stimulus was projected by the afferent path already outlined to Ammon's horn. After sufficient libido was generated it would discharge through the efferent path via the fornix with sufficient strength to break out of this circuit and find motor expression in an orgiastic epileptiform attack by way of the will paths outlined in Figure 5.

This is a most instructive case, first because it demonstrates that the orgasm is a central process, and second because it supports the idea that Ammon's horn is the source of libido and thus of feeling. But equally important is the fact that the cortical area representing the sexual organs and the cortical area to which the will might project are adjacent and thus could both be stimulated by the will.

The situation of this unfortunate woman somewhat resembles a compulsion neurosis which, it will be remembered, was explained as a reaction of the will to maternal restraints. When the mother interdicts masturbation or sexual expression as bad and the child identifies negatively with her, then at maturation it may react against this restraint by behavior which seeks pleasure in sexual badness, whether or not the sexuality is satisfied. In this case the stimulus would arise in the primitive will, i.e., in the mammillary

---

[45] Brodal, *loc. cit.*

FIG. 8 Diagram to illustrate hippocampal connections

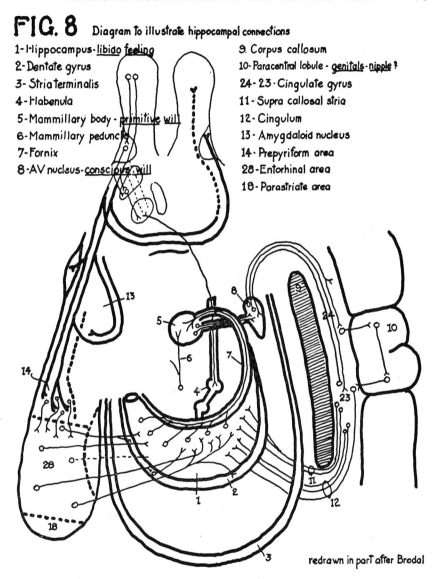

1- Hippocampus- libido feeling
2- Dentate gyrus
3- Stria terminalis
4- Habenula
5- Mammillary body - primitive will
6- Mammillary peduncle
7- Fornix
8- AV nucleus- conscious will

9. Corpus callosum
10- Paracentral lobule - genitals-nipple ?
24- 23 - Cingulate gyrus
11- Supra callosal stria
12- Cingulum
13- Amygdaloid nucleus
14- Prepyriform area
28- Entorhinal area
18- Parastriate area

redrawn in part after Brodal

body which would project sexual ideas to Area 24, and these in turn would stimulate Ammon's horn via the cingulum, whereas in the other case the stimulus would arise in the paracentral lobule simulating sexual intercourse.

The attacks to which this woman was subjected must have been accompanied by great guilt feeling because any libidinous will content causes guilt unless it can be justified by the superego. They occurred, then, in spite of her opposing will. The struggle against them would then be one of the will against libido, the conflict which is the basis for all the psychological aberrations. The denial, which is fundamental in the early development of the psychoneuroses, is of feeling, or, in other words, sublimated libido. This denial is accomplished by withdrawing the positive libidinous projections onto the object and projecting oral sadismus in their place. And this sadismus we have identified with the opposing will which found its anatomic counterpart in the DM nucleus; this we have shown might find cortical expression through the extrapyramidal system while the conscious will might find its expression through the pyramidal system. In the adult when the will hardens, i.e., becomes more sadistic, motor expression through the extrapyramidal system would predominate and overcome the feeling component of the conscious will entirely. If action resulted it would be antagonistic. This phase can scarcely be maintained permanently in most persons because of the guilt reaction that ensues, and then the opposing will turns into the ego structure as previously described to restrain the primitive will. Normally a varying amount of feeling would emerge from Ammon's horn, join with the primitive will, and become a part of the conscious will (in the AV nucleus). This feeling would then modify the sadismus in the opposing will and in this sense might be said to relax the tension caused by the opposing will (the extrapyramidal motor system). It is a normal component of the conscious will. But increased inordinately, it may form so large a part of the conscious will as to subjugate the opposing will, as in the case described above.

It may be well to indicate here that denial of feeling by the conscious will (the AV nucleus) may be justified anatomically. For Ingram's diagram of hypothalamic connections, Figure 4, shows connections passing from it via the mammillothalamic tract to the mammillary body (the primitive will) into which the fornix fibers debouch.

There is then a continual interplay between the will and feeling in the sense described above, the will necessarily overcoming feeling at one time and in turn being overcome by it at another. It is thus of extreme interest to consider whether this denial of the will by feeling is not directly related to the supressor bands described in the cerebral cortex. For Area 24, to which we have shown that the will might be projected, is a suppressor area and sends association fibers to Areas 6 and 4s, which is also a suppressor area. When feeling is strong in the will it might then effect Area 4s and cause relaxation of the muscles supplied by Area 6. But this must wait until other connections by which libido could be distributed from Ammon's horn have been discussed.

Ammon's horn and its descending connections.—The explanation given above shows that Ammon's horn is strategically and centrally placed to act as a source of libido and, through the connection from the AV nucleus to the paracentral lobule, as a stimulus to erotic sensations and to the orgasm. But it is equally important to show its possible connections with the genitals themselves so as to give them participation in the orgasm. Most of the fornix fibers terminate in the medial mammillary nucleus from which they *ascend* to the thalamus as already described. But others reach the lateral mammillary nucleus from which, along with fibers from the medial nucleus, they *descend* via the mammillotegmental tract.[46] Still other fornix fibers pass into the stria medullaris, reach the habenula, then the interpeduncular nucleus via the fasciculus retroflexus, and so pass caudally to the brain stem. Fornix fibers also pass to the hypothalamus and preoptic areas. Now the preoptic area is notably parasympathetic and we have seen that descending connections from the pars magnocellularis to the hypothalamus exist. And it has already been indicated that parasympathetic impulses probably pass to the brain stem via one of the periventricular systems. It seems likely therefore that these descending parasympathetic impulses meet the supposedly libidinous impulses from Ammon's horn descending by the mammillotegmental tract at some lower level. This would complete a somatic circuit through the genital tract and back via the mammillary peduncle to the medial hypothalamic nuclei and up to the DM nucleus. Since engorgement of the genitals is brought about by the parasympathetic this circuit would permit their preparation and associate genital activity with that of Ammon's horn in the orgasm.

Ammon's horn only indirectly connected with olfaction.—Modern staining methods have shown that on removal of the olfactory bulb in the experimental animal the fibers of the lateral root of the olfactory tract terminate not in Ammon's horn but in the prepyriform area and the periamygdaloid cortex, though some pass to the medial group of amygdaloid nuclei and a few to the central amygdaloid nucleus.[47] But cells in the prepyriform area send their axones to the entorhinal area which, as Area 28, constitutes most of the hippocampal gyrus in the human. In this area are cells whose axones project to Ammon's horn, the more medial by the alvear, the more lateral by the perforant path. There is then an indirect connection between the olfactory tract and Ammon's horn. If Ammon's horn is assumed to be the source of libido the function of these indirect connections now becomes quite understandable. For the main stimulant to libido in experimental animals such as the dog and rabbit is olfactory and comes from the genitals of the female. The entorhinal area in these animals would then be discriminatory and send impulses to the hippocampus only when the male detects the odor of estrus.

Ammon's horn stimulated visually in man.—In humans, at least in those of our time, such a positive stimulus from the prepyriform to the entorhinal area and Ammon's horn does not exist, unless a touch of perfume behind

[46] Brodal, *op. cit.*, p. 214.
[47] Fulton, *Phys. N.S.*, p. 332.

the ear can be considered erotic. On the other hand an unpleasant olfactory stimulus would certainly act negatively on the source of libido. Indeed, Rank believes that the feminine cult of beauty and cleanliness of body and clothing results from a positive identification with the early maternal restraints in regard to cleanliness of the perineal region. The strongest positive stimulus to libido, apart from direct physical contact, is now visual, and it is therefore of great interest to consider by what path visual impulses might reach the entorhinal area and so stimulate Ammon's horn.

The inferior longitudinal fasciculus is described[48] as a large bundle which runs through the entire length of the temporal and occipital lobes; it is part of the external sagital stratum and consists chiefly of geniculocalcarine fibers. The fibers of this bundle are actually shown to enter the hippocampal gyrus and to come into close relation with the tangential fibers found there as well as in the hippocampus in man.[49] It seems very likely then that this bundle forms the path by which visual impulses might reach the entorhinal cortex and so stimulate Ammon's horn to function. In addition, Area 23, the sensory portion of the cingulate gyrus, has association fibers with Areas 18–19[50] and these might permit visual images or visual memories to be taken up by the will.

The relation of libido to feeling and to affect in general.—It was stated above in discussing the relation between will and feeling that feeling was derived from libido. This idea of the sublimation of libido, first promulgated by Freud, must now be elaborated somewhat so as to form a basis for further discussion of the suppressor bands and the basal ganglia.

The writer has previously indicated that the pars magnocellularis of the DM nucleus might be responsible for the painful punishment inflicted on human beings by the superego: its projection toward the orbital surface might cause the latter to react in a way which the individual would perceive as painful guilt unless he could justify it as righteous anger. On the other hand, a libidinous content in the primitive will may cause pleasure but only when this content can be justified by the superego. Pain or anger on the one hand, pleasure on the other, are both affects, the first two on the negative side, the second on the positive. But each involves participation of the other. In the first instance there is a lesser participation of libido, though psychic pain at times is pleasurable; in the second there must be some participation of the opposing will (the DM nucleus) as restraint if the pleasure is not to become painful. Affect thus involves participation of both the negative and positive sides of the personality.

Affect and its expression in speech and music.—Speech and music are

---

[48] Ranson and Clark, *op. cit.*, p. 274.
[49] *Ibid.*, p. 287.
[50] Brodal, *op. cit.*, p. 215.

both methods of expression of the personality. Each may run the entire gamut of affect. The urge to death, the tragic poignancy of the sense of guilt, self-frustration of the will and libido are all painful punishments dealt out by the dreaded superego on one side. The crude primitive and narcissistic orgiastic satisfaction of libido by the egoist, the sexual love for a person of the other sex, the tender love of a parent for the child, the exquisite finer feelings of beauty evoked by the natural world about us, all represent gradations of development of libido on the other side. Both sides seek and find expression in speech and music.

Reciprocal relation between positive and negative affect.—But there is a reciprocal relation between crude orgiastic satisfaction on the one hand and the devastating painful sense of guilt on the other. This relation is amply demonstrated by the manic-depressive, whose very diagnosis points to the nature of his illness.

Development of crude affect into finer feeling.—Much of this appears in the psychotherapeutic situation. For it is confusion, suffering, and a sense of personal responsibility that brings the neurotic to the therapist. Many have often thought of suicide; all express their suffering by tears and speech; all seek to find release in spiritual growth, which, of course, is what they must experience. The dreams of this period often portray their plight in allegorical, religious pictures in which the cross plays a part. As they find some measure of expression and acceptance of the opposing will their spiritual growth begins and a sense of well-being appears. The first really positive will expressions in the woman are usually accompanied by a tremendous upsurge of feeling depicted in sexual terms in her dreams though she herself is conscious only of positive affect. This fact shows conclusively that positive affect is a veiled form of libido. If she has previously masturbated the crude narcissistic libido heretofore projected downward now passes upward and is affixed to the male object in her ego structure. Even when her previous sex life has been satisfactory, i.e., when she has responded with an orgasm, she now takes on a new attitude toward the man: she becomes womanly instead of the mere woman she was. If she bears a child the libido becomes a new tenderness toward a new object in a new and different object relationship. In other words, the crude libido develops by accretions of delicate nuances of meaning and feeling. It follows a pattern similar to that of the will, is subject to the same restraining effect of the superego through negative identification, may be arrested at the oral stage in the homosexual. In short, it contributes feeling to the will and might be distributed with it throughout the cerebrum.

Distribution of affect.—This understanding of feeling as developing out of libido might give new meaning to the progressive development of Ammon's horn in the phylogenetic ascent of mammals. But it also makes the feeling of well-being that appears characteristically in the psychotherapeutic situation understandable. And the wide distribution of fornix fibers, already noted, to the soma, the hypothalamus, the thalamus, and cortex would then become significant. For throughout the mammalian series they would distribute the sense of well-being to all parts of the organism.

In this connection the fibers ascending to the pars magnocellularis from the medial nuclei of the hypothalamus as the tract of Clark and Boggon[51] should find special mention. For while the finer connections between the hypothalamic nuclei still remain to be determined it is possible that this tract conducts libidinous energy to the DM nucleus via the fornix and the hypothalamus and thus to Areas 9, 10, 11, and 12, i.e., to the cortical representation of the personality. Throughout the early development of the ego, restraint of the will by the opposing will is brought about by identification with the mother. This restraint operates either as a damming back of the opposing will because of positive identification or as suppression of the opposing will by the superego because of negative identification. The latter is painful and indicates a suppression of well-being, i.e., of libido in the sense of its relation to feeling given above. Since this suppression would operate through fibers descending from the pars magnocellularis and terminating presumably in the medial hypothalamic nuclei, psychic pain might well be caused by preventing the distribution of libido to the DM nucleus. The tract of Clark and Boggon would thus act somewhat as a barometer of well-being; in phases of good will it would distribute libido to the whole personality; in painful phases of ill will the passage of this libido and/or feeling would be denied.

The structure of Ammon's horn in man shows a greater development and differentiation than that of the monkey and chimpanzee but the various portions into which it has been divided—the parasubiculum, presubiculum, prosubiculum, hippocampus proper, and dentate gyrus—are merely convenient anatomic divisions to which no special significance can be attached.

Ammon's horn as a possible source of both will and libido.—Heretofore, the present writer has assumed that the mammillary body represented the primitive will and Ammon's horn libido. But this gives a striking anatomic disproportion between the two structures which is entirely out of line with the clinical facts. For the human will is equally as definite an entity as libido. Indeed, neurotic patients are found whose problem seems to lie entirely in the field of the will and who claim that their sex life is quite normal. And since the will is subject to the same developmental influences as the libido and shows similar gradations as to strength and quality it would seem probable that its structure would be more complex than that of the mammillary

---

[51] Fulton, *Phys. N.S.*, p. 450.

nucleus. For the latter seems to represent a mere crossroad, so to speak. Ammon's horn presents two portions: the hippocampus proper and the dentate gyrus. Most fibers in the perforant path enter the hippocampus, a few the dentate gyrus; most fibers in the alvear path enter only the hippocampus. But the dentate gyrus and the hippocampus are connected by fibers from the dentate gyrus. Through the connections from the more medial portion of the entorhinal area via the alvear path it would be possible to stimulate Part 1 of the hippocampus and not the dentate gyrus. But stimulation from the more lateral part of Area 28 via the perforant path would stimulate both hippocampus and dentate gyrus. Is it not possible then that the hippocampus represents the will and the dentate gyrus the libido? Stimulation by the alvear path would thus arouse the will, stimulation by the perforant path both will and libido, and since the libido must be powered by the will this distribution of fibers by the perforant path to both would be understandable.

But both will and libido are autonomous and need no stimulus to be aroused. This is evident in the strong-willed person who seeks and finds an object for his creative activity entirely apart from any libidinous expression. To him, indeed, the intimate connections between the will and libido, which would be paralleled by the connections between the dentate gyrus and the hippocampus, would hinder the free creative operation of the will. This would make it necessary for him to shunt the will circuit through Areas 24 and 23 and back to the AV nucleus of the thalamus and so eliminate stimulation of the hippocampus via the paracentral lobule and cingulum.

Rationalization of libido or will.—The two circuits previously described are arranged so that either the will or the libido may operate separately. A compulsion neurotic whose psychological development is incomplete in the sense that he reacts to the maternal restraints with sexual badness might continually project sexual ideas to Area 24 and be almost completely overcome by guilt: he is narcissistic and rationalizes his libido. On the other hand, an unscrupulous businessman by denying his feeling for others might keep Area 24 so full of schemes for unfair monetary advantage that he is impelled to act on them: he is rationalizing his will. This rationalization of the will, or self-deception, is the commonest of human failings and occurs to a greater or lesser extent in all of us. The individual who rationalizes himself not only suspects he is guilty but knows he is guilty; he excuses himself because he sees everyone doing the same thing. He differs from the neurotic only in that he is less self-aware, has less severe guilt feelings, and so is able to live with his guilt.

Ammon's horn and the pituitary.—In discussing the hypothalamus as an anatomic representative of the instinctual id reasons have been given to suppose that the pituitary secretions are under the control of the psyche and that the constellation of the will forces and the superego influences the development of the sexual apparatus and its function. Here it remains to point out that fornix fibers pass to the hypothalamus and preoptic area and so might contribute libido to the pituitary during the developmental period too. The psyche would thus be primarily in control of the sexual function and the pituitary act as its agent through control of the development of the sexual apparatus. The impotence of the neurotic when he attempts intercourse would be primarily psychic. That is to say, he has not overcome the maternal restraints at the Oedipus stage and fears the female genitalia (vagina dentata); when alone he may have full erections. However, continued denial of the will seems to result in gradual physical deterioration; many who end up as alcoholics fall into this category and secondary failure of the pituitary secretions might play a part in this deterioration.

The question as to expression in action or speech.—We may continue the above discussion about Ammon's horn and the two circuits described by indicating that with either circuit the impulse may be put into action. This would be done by projection of the will alone or of the will and libido from the AV nucleus of the thalamus to the VL nucleus and motor cortex by way of the connections shown in Figure 5, or it would be put into speech by the same path with substitution of the VPM for the VL nucleus. The question as to whether speech or action is used will depend on how primitive the organization of the individual is. The more primitive one will tend to resort at once to action, the more advanced to speech. But beyond this decision lies another: whether or not to express the impulse at all. Here a still further degree of organization is needed. And this implies reflection which depends on the relative strength of the biological self, here represented by Ammon's horn and the mammillary body, and the social self, here represented by the DM nucleus. For when the biological self is stronger the tendency is to rationalize the will and to resort at once to action. And when the social self is stronger the tendency is for the reaction time of the will to be lengthened; the impulse would then pass to Area 24, but action, if it followed at all, would do so only after reflection (which is to say, only when it could be approved by the personality, and so eventually by the superego).

This question of the relative strength of the social and biological selves suggests at once Jung's broad division of personalities into two main types: the introvert and the extrovert, the former representing predominance of the social self and the latter predominance of the biological self. The comparison is very apt. Furthermore, the present writer's conception of the biological self as including both will and libido is quite in line with Jung's spiritual conception of libido as including much more than the sexual urge.

The origin and expression of fear.—The statement has already been made that oral sadismus might be suppressed by the infant because of fear of the mother's authority, or that it might dam back under the influence of her love. If one considers the power of this authority and adds to it an increment of irritation or sadismus which she often projects onto him in situations which try her patience it is easy to see that this suppression through fear might occur.

Its first beginning at weaning time is accompanied by withdrawal of the positive projections and denial of the mother. In normal persons this denial is soon overcome but in the strong-willed psychoneurotic it is increased during toilet training and continued at puberty so that the negative identification predominates and the positive plays a relatively minor part. This makes for great difficulty at the Oedipus stage when the boy's maternal restraints must be shifted to the father so as to make the mother once more the object of his positive libidinous projections. For the early fear of the mother's authority which has made her his superego now appears as an obstacle to this shift onto the father and keeps the boy at the narcissistic stage. At the Oedipus stage the fear which first arose on the negative side appears on the positive side as fear of positive expression. When projected to the face area of the cortex via the VPM nucleus this fear might mark the facial expression and speech; when projected to the motor cortex via the VL nucleus it might make action timid and indecisive or else entirely prevent action. Under these circumstances the immature neurotic individual often makes an effort to overcome the fear by increasing the amount of sadismus in the opposing will; he speaks and acts determinedly but feels shaky because of guilt feeling and of the antagonism he feels he arouses in others; he is ashamed to acknowledge this to himself and attempts to build up his ego by additions of narcissism which only make him more vulnerable to the resentment he causes in others. This fear is always seen clearly in the psychoneurotic situation but is ameliorated, covered, or replaced by libido as the relationship progresses.

It is thus possible to see that *neurotic* fear arises in connection with the opposing will and results from suppression of its sadistic expression by the maternal superego. In anatomical terms this means that the energy of the pars magnocellularis would be turned back through its connection with the medial hypothalamic nuclei as *fear* and that this would arrest or impede the development of the primitive will. In the neurotic this fear has been incompletely overcome and finds expression in the cortex as already described.

But it is also possible to see that *actual* fear arising from circumstances in the outer world would have substantially the same effect: the events would reach the DM nucleus by its connections with the eyes and ears, and overwhelm the pars magnocellularis (as the maternal superego does in the neurotic); this would then turn inward to affect the conscious will through the hypothalamus and its expression through the cortex. Thus fear, while

FIG. 9 Diagram of "suppressor" areas found in brain of chimpanzee and presumed to exist in that of the human. Feeling, as a component of the conscious will, is here supposed to be projected to these areas where it mollifies the sadistic opposing will in its transcortical passage caudad. Hardening of the will would overcome this feeling component. From these "suppressor" areas feeling is projected to the caudate whence it may pass either to the reticular formation to mollify the action of the medullary and spinal centers or to the feed-back mechanism for rein-forcement.

LEG

ARM

FACE

redrawn after Bucy

84

arising on one side of the ego structure, that connected with the DM nucleus, would find expression on the other, that connected with the AV nucleus.

At the cortical level, then, fear accompanying the conscious will would contend with the sadismus of the opposing will: the normal person would be able through experience to determine whether or not he could increase his sadismus so as to overcome it or whether he ought to flee; the neurotic because of greater fear accompanying his immature and primitive will might attempt to use the same mechanism but would almost certainly fail.

The Suppressor Bands and the Denial Mechanism

Four "suppressor" bands have been demonstrated by the strychnine method in the chimpanzee (see Fig. 9) and each of these has been shown to cause "suppression" of electrical activity in other cortical areas tested. To bring out a possible relation between these bands and the clinical facts of denial it will be necessary to question more closely what is meant by "suppression." In the cerebellum a different term is applied though apparently meant to indicate the same process. Thus it has been demonstrated that suitable stimulation of the dentate nucleus *inhibits* motor response to cortically induced movements such as contraction of the extensor carpi or the knee jerk;[52] and by inhibition here is meant a diminution in the height of the contraction. Stimulation of the fastigial nucleus on the other hand causes *facilitation* of these movements in the sense of increasing the height of the contraction. And either effect could be brought about from the same focus of stimulation depending on the frequency of stimulation of the anterior lobe of the cerebellum. It is indicated that the process in the cerebrum and in the cerebellum are of the same nature.[53] That is to say, the paleocerebellum from which the *inhibition* originates has an effect similar to the "suppressor" bands. Brodal, too, states that the effect of stimulating Area 24 is to *relax* the musculature supplied by Area 6, not to suppress it.[54]

This question of definition is raised because the clinical facts of denial suggest that the action of the suppressor bands might be to relax the musculature in the sense used by Brodal or to diminish the strength of the contraction in the sense of the response to stimulation of the dentate nuclei of the cerebellum and not necessarily to suppress all activity.

The clinical facts are that hardening of the will from increased sadismus overcomes feeling, whereas increase in the amount of feeling (libido) causes a softening of the will. If the term "suppression" can be used to indicate a lessening of the height of contraction or a mollification of tension, then a good

52 Fulton, *Phys. N.S.*, p. 521.
53 *Ibid.*, Fig. 126, p. 495.
54 Brodal, *op. cit.*, p. 215.

case can be made out for identifying the "suppressor" bands as cortical areas where the opposing will, as represented by the DM nucleus, and the feeling content of the conscious will meet in continual interplay.

Since these suppressor bands were demonstrated in the chimpanzee, whose brain so closely resembles that of the human, a portrayal of these "clinical facts" in this animal would go a long way toward proving the correctness of this thesis. For this proof we may return to the case of the chimpanzee, "Becky," previously discussed. She was an affectionate adolescent female on whom extensive experiments were made. She was given difficult problems to solve and co-operated fully up to the point where "temper tantrums" resulted from her failure to solve a problem. Then she "rolled on the floor, beat the cage, defecated and urinated" when she made a mistake.[55] It seems evident that affection and co-operation are manifestations of feeling and so represent this component of the conscious will. Frustration of this will caused by intellectual inability to accomplish a difficult task caused a reaction on the part of the opposing will; it escaped the restraining effects of the superego established by positive identification and showed itself by the "temper tantrums" described. Is this not a clear demonstration of the same overcoming of feeling by increase of sadismus and hardening of the will that we have described as a clinical fact in human beings?

A reaction that suggests the complete cessation of motor activity implied by the term "suppression," i.e., limits it to positive supporting reactions, has been observed by the writer in wild animals much less developed than chimpanzees. When one comes suddenly upon wild deer over the brow of a hill their first reaction to the sight and sound of the approaching car is complete arrest of all movement and fixation of gaze upon the object. This arrest of movement might be called an overcoming of their previous *feeling* of well-being and so illustrate to a certain extent the principle of interplay between opposing will and feeling. But the chimpanzee, who is nearer to man in the line of phylogenetic ascent of mammals, would illustrate it much more clearly.

One cannot fail to connect the arrest of all movement just described in wild animals with the projection of fear to the cortex from its origin in the DM nucleus via connections with the outer world. For it has been shown in the previous discussion of the origin of fear that this arises on one side of the ego structure but is manifested in the other. The sudden arrest of all movement would then represent the "suppression" by fear of motor activity described by the physiologists in connection with Area 4s. But fear would also alert the eye muscles in Areas 19 and 8 by directing the gaze toward the object ("suppression" of eye movements) and alert the somatic sensory apparatus in Area 2s by decreasing its sensitivity to somatic sensation. The "suppressor" bands in wild animals might thus be satisfactorily explained

[55] Fulton, *Phys. N.S.*, p. 456.

as cortical areas sensitive to fear arising from stimuli from the outer world.

In human beings we have described "neurotic" fear as having an origin and manner of expression similar to that of "actual" fear. Since the will of the neurotic is primitive and narcissistic and therefore accompanied by fear, it seems possible that in him the normal mollification of tension in the "suppressor" bands is supplanted by the more primitive "suppressing" action just described in wild animals and that he attempts to deny or overcome this by increasing the sadismus in the opposing will.

In Area 4s the interplay between the opposing will and feeling would best be shown by mollification of motor tension by feeling. This might be illustrated by the calming effect of a prolonged warm bath on a "nervous" person. In Areas 8s, 2s, and 19s it would best be shown in the overcoming of feeling by the opposing will. A frigid woman, for example, would illustrate a denial of feeling in the labia and vagina (Area 2s) by the opposing will; or a hysterical anesthesia would illustrate denial of feeling in an extremity in the same "suppressor" band. In Area 19s denial must take into consideration the theories developed in connection with the function of the temporal lobe to be described later. But it may be stated here that visual impulses from the outer world are postulated to be correlated with auditory impulses from the outer world in their passage forward by way of the inferior longitudinal fasciculus to the temporal tip where they meet an accessory superego and the amygdala representing feeling. The impulses (of sight and hearing) then return to Area 19 whence they are projected cephalad to the prefrontal lobe (character) by way of the inferior occipitofrontal fasciculus. If, then, feeling is projected to Area 19s and serves to maintain a sense of well-being and equanimity, disturbing or frightening impulses from the outer world perceived through the temporal lobe would, on returning to Area 19s, cause instant alarm and arouse the activity of the sadistic opposing will which might attempt to deny them. Thus, for example, the writer has seen a strong-willed, frigid woman fall to the floor while quarreling with her husband and cry out: "I cannot see." Her momentary blindness was a denial in Area 19s of the incoming stream of visual impulses from the temporal lobe, her fall the result of a suppression by the superego of her hatred and its effect through the ego structure on the primitive will. In Area 8s the denial of feeling by the will would be manifested by turning the gaze aside. This might be illustrated by observations made by the writer during a daily walk through a park. The paths here are narrow and only occasionally does one pass another person. These may almost be classified by their response to a friendly glance in their direction. Middle-aged or older persons generally respond with a friendly greeting. But younger persons both male and female not only often keep their gaze straight ahead but actually turn it away in another direction. This constitutes a denial of feeling: these young persons fearfully deny an interchange of feeling through the eyes. There are sexual implications in this denial. These younger persons are more narcissistic; their sexual curiosity is more easily aroused and therefore must be denied. This denial would arise in the character, Areas 9, 10, 11, and 12, and be achieved by turning the glance aside through Area 8.

There is then some clinical observation which shows that denial of feeling by the will may occur in so-called normal persons as well as in the neurotic. Denial thus varies in degree all the way from the concealment of his genitalia with a loin cloth by the primitive to the denial of the female genitalia in consciousness by the male neurotic. The evidence presented shows that this denial might be connected with the so-called suppressor bands.

In recapitulation one may say that (1) the feeling content of the normal conscious will mollifies the tension in the opposing will caused by increased sadismus, or there is phasic interplay between the two, and (2) the neurotic conscious will contains a greater amount of fear, and the sadismus in the opposing will increases to overcome this so that no real manifestation of feeling can occur; the denial might take place in the suppressor bands of the cortex.

Area 24 and the Fate of the Individual

One sees readily that the area including Ammon's horn, the mammillary body, the mammillothalamic tract, the AV nucleus, the cingulate gyrus, and the paracentral lobule might be the scene of operation of much of our being, our thinking, and our feeling. The fate of an individual might depend on what would be projected to Area 24. In children and particularly in boys it is obvious that the material projected to the will area is mostly a reaction to earlier maternal restraints; they scamper up and down the street armed with toy pistols and decorated with bandanas and cowboy boots in imitation of "bad men." If because of earlier events this reaction to maternal restraints is carried into the sexual field in adolescence serious results may ensue. In young adult life the future of the individual is often determined by the "reality" of the projection, i.e., by the degree to which the impulses originating in the primitive will have previously been influenced by the restraints of the opposing will and its connections with outer reality. Negative identification with these restraints may impede or arrest the development of the primitive will so as to make the individual neurotic, perverted, or psychotic: the projection to Area 24 is debased. The creative individual, however, may react against the restraint by projecting an idealized version of what should be, instead of what is, and this constitutes true creative activity. What is projected is in turn influenced by the relative strength of the opposing will (DM nucleus) and the primitive will (mammillary body). When the opposing will is stronger the individual is more likely to become neurotic under adverse conditions but may be helped by treatment to a "normal" state. He may be able to achieve this state for himself if he is able to justify his will by creative activity. When the primitive will is the stronger, and under adverse conditions, the individual may become creative in a negative sense. That is, his activity may become criminal.

The Suppressor Bands, the Caudate Nucleus, the Reticular Formation, and the Id

The suppressor areas have fiber connections to the caudate nucleus as well as to the reticular formation, and the caudate nucleus also projects to the reticular formation (Fig. 10). The inhibiting, or better, mollifying effect of feeling would thus be transferred to lower levels in the brain stem where it would act on the spinal reflexes. But the caudate nucleus terminates in the amygdala, which in experimental animals has been shown to act as a "funnel through which inhibiting influences . . . exert a suppressing action on brain stem mechanism." The neck of this inhibitory funnel is said to pass by way of the ventromedial nuclei of the hypothalamus.[56] This would bring the mollifying effects of feeling into the instinctual id. Indeed, sham rage brought about by other means in cats has been shown to be prevented so long as the "amygdala, the hippocampal formation and the cortical field of the pyriform lobe had been left intact."[57]

The Motor Cortex, the Lenticular Nuclei, and the Substantia Nigra

Areas 4 and 6 both project to the putamen and globus pallidus and the latter projects by way of the ansa lenticularis to the substantia nigra (see Fig. 9). Since Areas 4 and 6 are here supposed to give motor expression to the opposing will and the conscious will together, when the will is hardened, i.e., is without feeling, the lenticular nuclei would serve to conduct these impulses to the substantia nigra. The function of the substantia nigra is said to be unknown[58] but exhibition of the will without feeling would obviously be facilitatory and suggests its connection with the bulbar facilitatory area,[59] with which it is largely coextensive. However, it seems probable that while feeling might influence the reticular formation so as to mollify spinal reflexes and the hardened will the bulbar facilitatory area so as to intensify postural reflexes, neither would act entirely alone except in special emergencies, such as combat, when the hardening would be necessary so as to deny entirely all feeling for the opponent.

[56] Fulton, *Phys. N.S.*, p. 245.   [57] *Ibid.*, p. 245.
[58] Ranson and Clark, *op. cit.*, p. 196.   [59] Fulton, *Phys. N.S.*, p. 495.

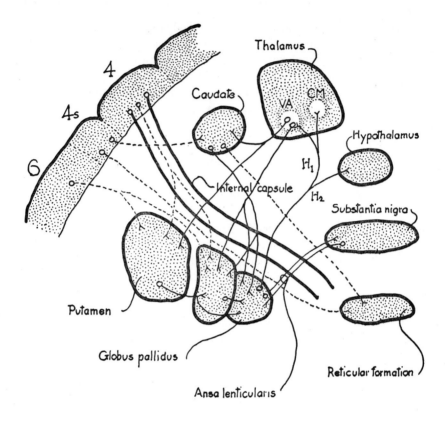

FIG.10 Diagram to illustrate inter-connections between basal ganglia & cortex.
The conscious will is projected to area 4, the opposing will to area 6; a part of each
then passes via the putamen and globus pallidus to the substantia nigra.
When the will hardens the opposing will predominates and the postural reflexes
are reinforced; when feeling predominates it is projected to area 4s and then
to the caudate and reticular formation where the spinal reflexes are mollified; but
this activation may also affect the globus pallidus.
Both sadismus and feeling may thus return via H_2 and H_1 to the thalamus
and be intensified by the feed-back mechanism which
the lenticular nuclei and
the thalamus   redrawn in part from Fulton
constitute.

Activation of Area 4s by the Thalamus

The tendency of this work has been to show that all the forces contributing to the psyche operate through the thalamus. It is here postulated that this principle can be applied to the suppressor strips and that these are activated by the feeling component of the conscious will through the ventral thalamic nuclei. This would form a circuit from the VL nucleus to Area 4s, caudate nucleus, globus pallidus, and back to the VL nucleus via the fields of Forel, which would mollify the motor tension caused by the will forces acting through Areas 4 and 6. And this circuit would be similar to that worked out experimentally in animals.[60]

Reinforcement of the Will by the Lenticular Nuclei and Thalamus as a Feed-Back Mechanism

The time element is very important in our psychic processes. For example, if a libidinous impulse arises in the mammillary nucleus of an immature young male, takes form as an idea in the AV nucleus, and is then projected to Area 24, it may remain in consciousness for some time and grow in intensity until the individual is impelled to act in such a way as to gratify it. The idea may be generated wholly narcissistically within the ego (autoeroticism) or it may result from association with a similarly immature young woman, the association being equally erotic to her. Circumstances being favorable, the longer the association the more likely it will be to arouse the libido, which may then seek outward expression in action, or at least in speech. The same sort of thing may, in an immature person, occur on the negative side. That is to say, an imagined grievance might be projected to Area 24—since the immature will may be sadistic along with the opposing will—and remain there for some time growing in intensity meanwhile until finally the individual feels impelled to take some spiteful action against the other party. His immature superego has allowed him to rationalize his antagonism. If he remains immature he continues to do this even later in life. The mechanism by which this occurs acts like a feed-back in that a part of the output returns to the source and gradually increases the output.

While this feed-back mechanism is evidently a will phenomenon it deals notably with content. That is to say, particular thoughts or variations of these thoughts continue to circle around and around and are either verbalized or pictured in consciousness. This concept indicates to the writer that this material might be connected with the VPM nucleus, which one might call a nucleus of expression; it projects to the face area and, as has been shown, to both its pyramidal and extrapyramidal portions.

[60] Fulton, *Phys. N.S.*, p. 492.

The present writer has been led to a consideration of the thalamus and lenticular nuclei as a structure to explain the elaboration and expression of this phenomenon. Connections pass from the thalamus, where the anatomic texts show them to originate in the ventralis anterior nucleus, and cross the internal capsule to the globus pallidus.[61] This VA nucleus is an association nucleus lying anterior to the remaining ventral nuclei. It not only has connections *to* the globus pallidus but receives connections *from* the globus pallidus via the fields of Forel.[62] This completes a circuit from the VA nucleus to the globus pallidus and back to the VA nucleus. The latter as an association nucleus has on its anterior end the AV nucleus, the supposed source of the conscious will, and on its posterior end the VL and VPM nuclei, which would have to do with expression of the will. But as we have seen, this mechanism deals particularly with verbalized expression, i.e., with content, and the VPM nucleus would therefore be the one primarily concerned in its operation and therefore included in the circuit.

The centromedian nucleus lies in and partly enclosed by the internal medullary lamina immediately subjacent to the DM nucleus and between it and the VPM nucleus from which it takes its shape. It, too, is an association nucleus and might well associate the DM nucleus on its medial superior surface and the VPM nucleus on its inferior lateral surface. It receives connections *from* the globus pallidus[63] but connections *to* the globus pallidus are not given. If to-and-fro connections to the globus pallidus *do* exist, as in the case of the VA nucleus, they would provide a second circuit from the thalamus to the globus pallidus and back to the thalamus, whereby sadistic or negative impulses might circle around and around gaining an added increment of sadismus from the DM nucleus each time. The VPM nucleus as the medium of expression of *content* would be included in the positive circuit originating in the VA nucleus as well as in the negative circuit originating in the DM nucleus. A feed-back mechanism would thus be provided for reinforcement of both positive and negative ideas by circulation between the thalamus and globus pallidus. When either one gained sufficient intensity it could find verbal expression through cortical projection from the VPM nucleus or expression in action through cortical projection from the VL nucleus. It is conceivable that the globus pallidus contributes to the gain in intensity by virtue of the motor-type cells of which it is composed.

These circuits would be similar to that just given on page 91 for mollification of motor tension but here the cortex and caudate would be excluded by the short circuit from the thalamus to the globus pallidus so as to permit thought without action. The necessary connections are shown in Figure 10.

---

[61] Ranson and Clark, *op. cit.*, p. 266.
[62] Fulton, *Phys. N.S.*, p. 269.
[63] *Ibid.*, p. 268.

The VPM Nucleus as the Origin of Speech and Magic

The VPM nucleus with its dual motor control of the medullary nuclei for the facial mechanism seems to the present writer perhaps the most important of the hierarchy of thalamic nuclei in human beings because it mediates speech. Since this nucleus might respond to either or to both phases of the will, speech might run the entire gamut of emotional expression; it is more than a mere method of communication because it may *affect* the feelings and actions of other persons and thus subject them to the will of the speaker. This effect is obvious in every phase of the life about us: through speech the labor leader willfully guides the actions of his union members because by their collective action he can provide increased material benefits for them and a richer living for himself; through speech the demagogue skillfully incites the passions of the crowd because he hopes to buy their votes by legislation which will benefit their material status and give him longer tenure; through speech the educator guides the thoughts and actions of his pupils so as to direct their will to knowledge and truth; through speech the priest induces in his congregation a beneficent mood of submission to and reverence for the collective superego. This subjection of others to the wishes of one person by word of mouth is characteristic of the strong-willed person and since he may bring them to his way of thinking and induce them to act out his wishes it seems like a kind of *magic*. Indeed, in primitive times spoken and written words *were magic* and the persons from whom they emanated were magic makers. In modern times strong-willed persons are still about and still work magic but may now be divided into categories as men of action and men of thought according to the relative strength of the primitive will and opposing will: the men of action still work their magic by the spoken word and these wonders may be either beneficent or malevolent according to whether their doctrine is for or against the collective superego; the men of thought still work their magic by speech but now by the written word and thought, and this again may be for or against the collective superego. The human will expressed in speech seems thus to be the source of magic but this idea is now rationalized in one way or another.

The possession of such a "magic" will is a problem in the neurotic because he represents an extreme development of modern man's self-awareness. He is secretly aware of this unreal magical quality in his will but his strong attachment to reality forces him to deny it even though this denial is the cause of his downfall. *He* cannot, like the labor leader, express his will and then deny it by asserting that what he does is not for himself but for his union; *he* cannot, like the demagogue, exert his will on the voters and then deny it by claiming that he aims only to help them. In short, the only way left for him is to express his will creatively in such a way as to allow it to reach the fullest possible development which his superego permits; and this usually means that he must subordinate his sexuality to other creative ideals. The extreme self-awareness of the neurotic brings him closer to reality by denying him the magic satisfaction of control of the actions of others; but it also denies him what most persons consider to be normal satisfactions and ways of will expression.

The Cerebellum

While the psychic forces under discussion in this book do not operate primarily in the cerebellum they most certainly enter prominently into its function: the fibers of the pyramidal tract which we have assigned to the conscious will give off collaterals which cross to the opposite side and terminate in the nuclei pontis; from these nuclei arise the fibers which form the brachium pontis or middle cerebellar peduncle, which supplies the neocerebellar portion of the cerebellar hemisphere. On the other hand many of the fibers from the extrapyramidal tract which we have assigned to the opposing will pass to the substantia nigra via the strionigral tract. The path from here to the cerebellar cortex is not known but it is supposed that the premotor cortical projections which influence postural mechanisms are associated primarily with the anterior lobe and the paleocerebellar mechanisms.[64] This association would bring them into relation with the proprioceptive impulses which reach the anterior lobe and the paleocerebellum via the ventral and dorsal spinocerebellar tracts. The smooth expression of the will forces in action would thus be made possible by synergy in the cerebellum of the action of voluntary muscles with proprioceptive information from the muscles and joints.

But the labyrinth and vestibular nuclei form another force which enters into the cerebellar picture through their connection with the flocculonodular lobe or paleocerebellum. The labyrinth, through the vestibular nuclei, reacts to the gravitational force of the outer world with impulses reaching the motoneurones in the anterior horn via the vestibulospinal tract. This gives automatic synergy to the motor apparatus so that the slightest change in the relation of the body to the earth's surface (such as the shifting of the weight from one foot to the other) is compensated for by a suitable readjustment of the postural muscles.

This automatism is proved by an experiment in which the brain stem of an experimental animal is severed above the level of the vestibular nuclei. This of course separates the source of voluntary activity from its means of expression in the soma but nevertheless results in decerebrate rigidity, i.e., allows unrestrained action of the vestibular nuclei on the postural muscles.

---

[64] Fulton, *Phys. N.S.*, p. 527.

In such a state of decerebrate rigidity, suitable stimulation of the anterior lobe of the cerebellum, which receives a large part of the proprioceptive impulses via the ventral spinocerebellar tract, results in relaxation of the postural musculature. The vestibular nuclei thus react to the outer reality of the gravitational force by inciting motor action, and the anterior lobe of the cerebellum to the inner reality of feeling (the sensory impulses from the muscles and joints) by inhibiting this motor action.

This unconscious and automatic reciprocal relationship between motor action and its inhibition by the anterior lobe of the cerebellum is mentioned here because it parallels so closely the conscious reciprocal relationship previously postulated between the opposing will, or DM nucleus, and the feeling component of the conscious will, or AV nucleus, which is here attributed to libido and the hippocampus. At this higher conscious level we find that the opposing will, or DM nucleus, by denying the feeling component of the conscious will, or AV nucleus, may react aggressively against the outer world by motor activity in which the extrapyramidal tract might play the major part. On the other hand, the activity of the conscious will, or AV nucleus, may be supplanted in large part by the activity of the mammillary nucleus, or primitive will, with its largely uncontrolled component of libido so that the opposing will, or DM nucleus, with its content of outer-world reality is almost completely denied and the motor apparatus loses most of its power to resist aggression from the outer world.

In recapitulation one might say that when the opposing will is allocated to the DM nucleus and the feeling component of the conscious will to the suppressor band (Area 4s) a reaction is found at the conscious level similar to that between the vestibular nuclei and the proprioceptive impulses reaching the anterior lobe of the cerebellum via the ventral spino–cerebellar tract at the unconscious level of the cerebellum; in both cases this reaction results in relaxation of the postural muscles.

Summary of the Interrelations of the Thalamic Nuclei and Their Cortical Connections

It was the conviction of the late Professor Grafton Elliott Smith that the key to the interpretation of the cerebral cortex lay in the thalamus[65] and the present work supports his opinion. Here in the pool of gray matter that forms its lateral and posterior portions, all the data from the outer and inner worlds reach a series of nuclei which are not only the termination of afferent systems but the beginning of efferent systems to the cortex; proprioceptive impulses from the cerebellum relay in the ventrolateralis, where impulses to the motor cortex find origin; sensory impulses from the soma relay in the ventro-

---

[65] *Ibid.*, p. 267.

posterolateralis, where impulses to the postcentral sensory cortex find origin ; sensory and proprioceptive impulses from the face relay in the ventroposteromedialis, where the motor impulses to the face area of the cortex find origin, and whence the sensory and motor impulses are projected to this face area ; sensory impulses from the optic nerves relay in the lateral geniculate, where visual impulses to the striate area find origin ; and sensory impulses from the auditory nerve relay in the medial geniculate, where impulses to the auditory cortex find origin. The common features of all these nuclei are that in each there is an interruption between the afferent and efferent impulse, that each lies in the pool of gray matter of the lateral and posterior mass, and that none of them are interconnected. The law of neurobiotaxis would indicate that all these nuclei were gathered together about a common source of control, and their common features have led the present writer to assume that this source of control was the will. For these common features seem to be the only possible explanation for the fact that the will may choose whether it is to be expressed passively in thought, to give particular attention to visual or auditory impulses, or to express itself in speech or action ; and a process of diffusion through the gray matter seems to be the only possibly way in which it might reach the necessary nuclei ; if fixed connections between the nuclei existed this would not be possible. In this sense, then, there is some freedom of the will : through the relays in the ventral nuclei it may select and direct the activities of the organism ; through the relays in the posterior nuclei, the geniculate bodies which are attached to the pulvinar, it may receive information and direct its attention to the outer world. Between the ventral nuclei and the pulvinar lies the lateralis posterior, which by the necessity of its situation must associate the data received from the outer world by the geniculates with action directed toward the outer world. The pulvinar has to-and-fro connections with Area 19, the lateralis posterior with the associative area of the parietal lobe ; through these to-and-fro connections the will might direct the *cortical* association of the incoming data and the *cortical* action toward the object in the outer world. If, as the writer has assumed, the primitive will reaches and becomes conscious in the anterior ventral nucleus, then it would have access by association through the ventralis anterior, and by diffusion through the entire pool of gray matter, to all the nuclei that relay in it.

But the conscious will is only one of the will forces and before it is expressed it unites with the opposing will. This is represented by the dorsalis medialis which for the most part is separated from the others by the medullary lamina. The union of the DM nucleus with the ventral and posterior nuclei might occur by association through the dorsolateralis which receives connections from the DM nucleus and distributes them to both the ventral group and the lateralis posterioris, as shown in Figure 5. Since the pars parvicellularis projects to the prefrontal lobe it would be the energy of the pars magnocellularis which is introduced into the sphere of influence of the anterior ventral, and both together would form what we call the will. The ventral and posterior nuclei might thus form a series to which the influence of the DM nucleus would be added, and this series would have connections with corresponding cortical areas which would make possible the control of these cortical areas by the will.

The character has been shown to be the product of the will and opposing will, its cortical representative being the prefrontal lobe, where the action patterns which constitute behavior must be established. *In action* it would find expression by impulses passing caudad transcortically toward the striate area and meet visual impulses passing cephalad transcortically in the associative area of the parietal lobe. But *in thought* character might function subcortically as it would in a dream because its nuclear representative is the pars parvicellularis of the DM nucleus which is shown in Figure 5 to receive sensory impulses from the outer world via the geniculate bodies.

Here, then, is an arrangement of the thalamic nuclei which uses their known spatial relations and their known connections so as to permit the two will forces to find cortical expression together, and which connects them with the hypothalamus by known afferent and efferent connections. The hypothalamus would in turn receive the hippocampal output of feeling and/or libido, which, on transmission to thalamic and cortical levels, would contend with sadismus for conscious control of the organism. The suppressor bands with their caudate connections would give an adequate explanation for this control through feeling by way of brain stem "suppression" and the lenticular nuclei an adequate explanation for this control through sadismus by way of brain stem "facilitation." Since the hypothalamus receives the impact of the pars magnocellularis through known connections and the mammillary body gives off descending as well as ascending connections, the will forces might be projected caudad through the hypothalamus to provide unconscious control of the organism. The lenticular nuclei and the thalamus acting together might form a feed-back mechanism which could act to reinforce the will. The arrangement of this diencephalic concatenation of nuclei and connections is entirely dependent on Rank's reduction of the psychic forces to a few relatively simple elements, i.e., on his ability to show that the will may find an infinite number of contents which may all be reduced to the same elemental forces; and the arrangement shows such agreement with the ego structure devised from the will psychology as to make it quite possible that the will actually uses these channels for expression. In any case this arrangement of nuclei and their connections, together with the conception of diffusion of will impulses through them, provides a useful hypothesis for clinical consideration and a basis for experimental work.

General Discussion

This attempt to interpret the psyche in anatomic and physiologic terms is presented with considerable misgiving because the present writer is neither an anatomist nor a physiologist. On the other hand, the lack of these qualifications may actually have been an advantage in this interpretation because it has enabled him to view the anatomic facts, previously worked out by others, impartially and entirely apart from the dedicated attitude toward experimental laboratory science so characteristic of workers in this field. The psychic mechanisms on which the ego structure depends could scarcely have been elucidated by laboratory means; they have been worked out nonetheless by experimental means, first by observation of the constantly recurring will phenomena in the psychotherapeutic situation, second by varying the conditions set by this situation until the constructive forces in the psyche could work themselves out to a favorable conclusion. That is to say, the facts on which the will psychology is based are derived from experimental procedures and to one kind of mind may be quite as valid as those obtained in a laboratory.

As already indicated, the diagram representing the ego structure was devised from ideas culled from both Rank's genetic psychology and his will psychology. Since the latter seems to have been in part a reaction to Freud's refusal to accept his ideas, and completely abandons his conception of libido as the basic source of feeling, there is necessarily some conflict between the will psychology and the diagram of it in this book. The present writer has included the libido idea in his diagram because it was impossible to find a satisfactory anatomic parallel without it. And when included it found a natural origin in the hippocampus, which Papez had already suggested as the source of feeling. With this the connections of the "suppressor" areas of the cortex with the caudate nucleus, and the relation of the caudate with the lenticular nuclei and with the brain stem seemed to fall naturally into place and made possible a conception of brain function which sets the existing structures in motion in a plausible way.

The lack of definite connections between the nuclei in the lateral and posterior masses of the thalamus and the conception that the will forces enter these nuclei at the synapse may invalidate the whole scheme for the laboratory scientist. But, as already pointed out, if definite anatomic connections did exist the reactions of the psyche would be as predictable as those in the spinal cord, whereas the contrary is true: there is so much variation in individuals that their reactions to external events can only be understood by reference to some such pattern as has been worked out in the ego structure. Since the presence of a cardio-inhibitory substance has been demonstrated in the perfusate from a frog's heart after vagus stimulation and the presence of a cardioaccelerator substance after sympathetic stimulation,[66] and since the conscious will has here been given a sympathetic origin and the opposing will a parasympathetic origin, one might speculate that chemical substances such as "sympathin" and "vagus substance" might effect conduction of the will impulses through the gray matter in the thalamus. But in any case uncertainty about the way in which these forces are conducted in the thalamus militates against acceptance of the writer's conception even if the anatomic connections given in Figure 5 be approximately correct.

While the parallel found between the diagram and the anatomic structure gives us no proof that this particular interpretation of psychiatric phenomena is the correct one, it nevertheless supports it. And while the interpretation of brain function here worked out gives us no proof that the brain actually operates in this manner it nevertheless affords a way in which it might operate. This has not heretofore been possible.

In concluding this discussion of the book the present writer would like to emphasize again that he presents it only as a first, necessarily uncertain, and speculative beginning in this difficult field, as a gross delineation of the psychic forces in structural form. Nevertheless he hopes that it may serve as a basis for clarification and objectification of psychological concepts and as a stimulus to new approaches for investigating the human brain.

The Temporal Lobe

The temporal lobe has received little mention here so far, the main reason being that it finds no counterpart in the ego structure devised from the will psychology. But if one considers not only the experimental findings in animals and the clinical study of this lobe in humans, but also its known connections with the frontal lobe and the principles of the will psychology, it is possible to develop a satisfactory theory of its function and to see that it plays a most important part in the relation of the individual to the outer world.

In this connection the following must be kept in mind: an important stretch of transitional cortex extends from the cingulate gyrus into the insula, posterior orbital gyrus, and the tip of the temporal lobe and is histologically discrete.[67] The cingulate gyrus (Fig. 11-B-24), it will be remembered, is the supposed projection area of the conscious will, and the feeling component of the will has been postulated to reach the cortex in the suppressor bands. These suppressor bands (Fig. 9) project to the caudate nucleus, the tail of which terminates in the amygdala situated near the temporal tip (Fig. 11-A-8); the mollifying or "supressor" effect of feeling and/or libido

[66] Fulton, *Phys. N.S.*, p. 230.
[67] *Ibid.*, p. 486.

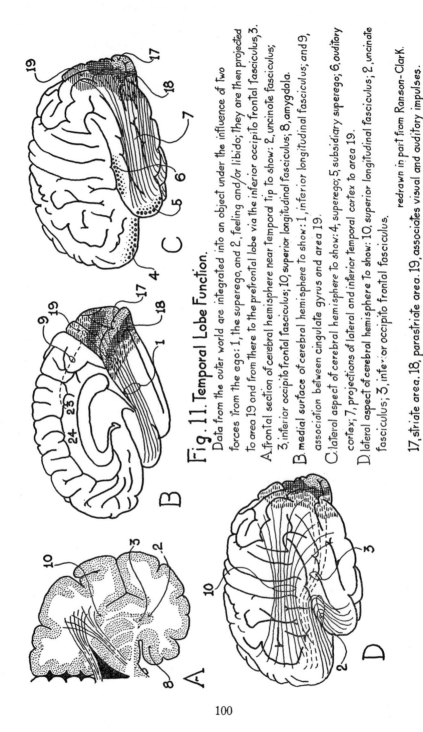

Fig. 11. Temporal Lobe Function.

Data from the outer world are integrated into an object under the influence of two forces from the ego: 1, the superego, and 2, feeling and/or libido; they are then projected to area 19 and from there to the prefrontal lobe via the inferior occipito frontal fasciculus, 3.

A. frontal section of cerebral hemisphere near temporal tip to show: 2, uncinate fasciculus; 3, inferior occipito frontal fasciculus; 10, superior longitudinal fasciculus; 8, amygdala.

B. medial surface of cerebral hemisphere to show: 1, inferior longitudinal fasciculus, and 9, association between cingulate gyrus and area 19.

C. lateral aspect of cerebral hemisphere to show: 4, superego; 5, subsidiary superego; 6, auditory cortex; 7, projections of lateral and inferior temporal cortex to area 19.

D. lateral aspect of cerebral hemisphere to show: 10, superior longitudinal fasciculus; 2, uncinate fasciculus; 3, inferior occipito frontal fasciculus.

17, striate area. 18, parastriate area. 19, associates visual and auditory impulses.

redrawn in part from Ranson-Clark.

would thus be transferred to the temporal lobe close to its tip. The orbital surface (Fig. 11-C-4), on the other hand, here forms what we have called the superego, and as such would normally restrain the biological self so as to make it conform to the ethical demands of the moral code. It reacts to sadistic expression of the opposing will with guilt feeling, and punishes such expression masochistically. But strychninization of the orbital surface activates the tip (Fig. 11-C-5) of the temporal lobe, and the cytoarchitectural structure of the temporal tip and the orbital gyrus is closely similar. Furthermore, marked respiratory and blood pressure changes can be evoked from the temporal tip as well as from the orbital surface;[68] and the two are connected by the uncinate fasciculus (Fig. 11-A-2). The hardening effect of sadismus and the mollifying effects of feeling on the will would thus be brought to bear on the activities of the temporal lobe.

Olfactory impulses reach the uncinate, or hippocampal gyrus (Fig. 8-28), from the prepyriform area anteriorly (Fig. 8-14), while visual impulses reach it from the parastriate area (Fig. 8-18) posteriorly. These visual impulses pass by way of the inferior longitudinal fasciculus (Fig. 11-B-1) which runs through the entire length of the temporal and occipital lobes.[69] The power to stimulate libido formation in the hippocampus was earlier attributed to these visual impulses in humans, while in experimental animals this power seemed clearly due to the odor of estrus. This gave to the uncinate gyrus some choice as to whether libido should be stimulated or not, and it is now suggested that this choice depends in part on the activity of the temporal tip and in part on the activity of the amygdala. The temporal tip would thus be a subsidiary moral authority taking its character from that of the main superego, and affecting or reacting to the impulses reaching the ego from the outer world through Area 19 (Fig. 11-B and -C). When the superego was severe and punishing, sexual impulses *within* the ego might be savagely suppressed and impulses relating to women's secondary sexual attributes reaching the temporal lobe from the *outer* world be interpreted as sinful. When the superego was immature and constituted mostly of maternal restraints it would be unable to cope successfully with the more infantile type of libido then projected from the primitive will to the suppressor bands, caudate, amygdala, and temporal lobe, where it would color the impulses from the outer world. An adolescent boy might then see all girls from a purely sexual standpoint and regard their rounded breasts and well-turned limbs as subjects for delighted but often guilty contemplation. For all these impulses from the outer world, except those of taste, are received by the temporal lobe: those from the olfactory nerve by way of the prepyriform area, those from the optic nerve by way of the inferior longitudinal

---

[68] Fulton, *Phys. N.S.*, p. 363.
[69] Ranson and Clark, *op. cit.*, p. 274.

fasciculus, and those from the auditory (and vestibular?) nerves by way of the auditory cortex on the inferior lip of the sylvian fissure (Fig. 11-C-6). Every possible aberration of the ego might thus effect the interpretation of these impulses.

The entire ventrolateral surface of the temporal lobe has been shown by strychnine studies to project posteriorly (Fig. 11-C-7) to Area 19, and is thus to be considered a visual association area.[70] The visual impulses would thus pass anteriorly by the inferior longitudinal fasciculus to meet with the auditory and olfactory impulses and the restraining influence of the temporal tip; the associated psychic product of sight, sound, and odor would then be projected back to Area 19. It has previously been postulated that this product was projected cephalad by way of the superior longitudinal fasciculus (Fig. 11-D-10) to meet impulses passing caudad transcortically from the prefrontal lobe (Fig. 7), the site of the personality, and associating them in the parietal lobe. But this idea of the rostral transcortical projection of the associated product of visual and auditory impulses via the superior longitudinal fasciculus can be only partially true for this reason: bilateral ablation of the temporal lobe results in psychic blindness. After extensive bilateral ablation of the temporal lobe monkeys are unable to recognize objects by sight (or touch). Normally they are terrified of snakes but after such an ablation handle them freely without fear; normally they select at once the edible objects from a series, but after this operation they are unable to do this and carry each to the mouth in turn to determine if it is edible; they even attempt to pick up a chalk mark among a series of objects.[71] This would indicate that the psychic meaning of the object reached the prefrontal lobe, the personality, by some path other than the superior longitudinal fasciculus to which, after the ablation, merely the visual outline remained to guide the will directing the use of the extremity. Since the inferior occipitofrontal fasciculus (Fig. 11-A and -D), is composed of long fibers passing along the ventrolateral border of the lentiform nucleus and joining the frontal and occipital lobes,[72] and would be destroyed in the extensive ablation of the temporal lobe described above, it might be presumed that it is this fasciculus which carries the psychic meaning cephalad to the personality and whose interruption causes psychic blindness.

Following symmetrical bilateral ablation of the temporal lobes in a trained baboon the animal behaves in an essentially normal manner; it is not deaf and recognizes the significance of spoken words, though it localizes poorly the direction from which the sound comes.[73] This is interesting in view of the assumption previously made that the relay in the medial geniculate re-

[70] Fulton, *Phys. N.S.*, p. 363.
[71] *Ibid.*, p. 361.
[72] Ranson and Clark, *op. cit.*, p. 274.   [73] Fulton, *Phys. N.S.*, p. 360.

ceives will impulses from the pool of gray matter in the posterior end of the thalamus, for it indicates that the auditory impulses might be perceived by the will at this point without projection to the auditory cortex in the temporal lobe (see Fig. 5). Though ablation of the auditory cortex does not result in deafness, blindness results from removal of the *occipital* lobe, which shows that the visual images could not be received by the will until *after* they had reached the visual cortex and returned to the relay in the *lateral* geniculate. It is of further interest that transcortical connections exist between the auditory cortex and the eye areas in Areas 8 and 19 so that both of these might be alerted by a sound and direct the gaze toward the object.[74]

There is experimental evidence which may be interpreted to show that the temporal tip, acting as a subsidiary restraining authority, has a suppressor effect on impulses from the outer world. Thus after isolating single nerve fibers of the acoustic nerve in the cat and stimulating them by sounds of different frequency and intensity, experimenters have found that in a single fiber a tone of one intensity may inhibit another tone presented concurrently, thus accounting for the phenomenon of tone masking.[75] This inhibition, or tone masking, might well originate in the suppressor action of the temporal tip. In any case mechanical interference in the auditory receptor was excluded as an explanation for it.[76]

It might well be the temporal lobe that is involved in such auditory hallucinations as were once exhibited by a patient seen some years ago. This was a woman with a mild form of schizophrenia who made a good recovery under psychotherapy but later had two psychotic episodes, one connected with threatened loss of her husband's affection, the other with his actual death. After the final date had been set she felt she could not get well unless she got rid of the "voices" she heard. If, as already postulated, the will normally projects the auditory impulses to the cortex by entering the circuit at the relay in the medial geniculate body, then it would be possible for the psychotic will to project itself to the auditory cortex through the same relay and thus simulate the "hearing of voices." This patient had carried her maternal restraints over into adult life and thus had an immature superego; her temporal tip might then have been similarly affected and unable to cope successfully with the organization by the psychotic will of stimuli from the outer world into aberrant psychic meanings.

It is now proposed to discuss, in terms of the theory developed above, the "dreamy states" first described by John Hughlings Jackson, and the interesting clinical work of Penfield on epileptiform seizures originating in the temporal lobe. But first some of the will psychology must be reviewed in order to make this discussion meaningful.

[74] *Ibid.*, p. 360.
[75] *Ibid.*, pp. 358–59.   [76] *Ibid.*, p. 359.

It will be remembered that the creative person was described as one whose primitive will overcame the (maternal) restraints of the opposing will, and who developed an ideal toward which he purposefully directed the activity of his conscious will; this was the creative person whose opposing will or social self overbalanced his biological self, the creative man of thought. But his opposite, the creative person whose biological self overbalanced his social self, tended to override the restraints of his opposing will and so, when his superego was mature, and his ideal therefore positive, consciously used the "magic" of his will to influence the behavior of others, not similarly endowed, toward his own high ideals; this was the creative man of action, the leader of other men. Both of these types have been the source of the creative evolution of Western man, the great mass of average men trailing along behind the ideas of the one and the actions of the other, and accepting this leadership because their own will was less powerful, their own superego less mature, and their own ego more receptive to outside influence.

But the creative person with the strong opposing will is often very self-aware and unless he firmly establishes his own superego and ideal may lead a troubled life. His tendency is then to use his creative will on himself in such a way as to inflate the image of himself he projects into Area 24. When young and naïve he may act on the assumption that this image is the correct one; he projects himself onto others as he wishes them to see him. But his perceptual faculties, which relate him to the outer world, his eyes and ears, receive this projected image reflected in the mirror and in the disbelieving eyes and attitude of those about him to whom he does not "ring true." The image thus returned to his ego through his perceptual faculties impinges on his superego and he is at once overcome with guilt and confusion; there is a gap between the image of himself that he has attempted to project outwardly and its reflection received by his eyes.

But if the person with the strong opposing will has used his creative power to further ethical ideals instead of monetary interests or biological impulses his integration may then give him sufficient self-confidence to accept the image of himself he sees reflected in his mirror, or even to accept the disbelief he sees reflected in the eyes of those about him. Copernicus, for example, must have had to make a great inner struggle to face courageously the disbelief he perceived in the eyes of the many accepting the Ptolemaic system. And Rank, himself, wrote of his discovery of the opposing will as neo-Copernican and indicated that he had been able to accept it only after much travail.

The neurotic, on the other hand, has been shown to be a strong-willed personality, who, because of untoward circumstances, has retained a maternal superego, denied his will through fear, and therefore projected a debased image of himself to Area 24; he despises himself. This image is projected outward onto others in spite of himself; he sees it reflected in his mirror and in the eyes of those about him; and this reflected image merely confirms and seems to make final the opinion he already has of himself, that he has no will at all.

These perceptual faculties might operate through the mechanisms of the temporal lobe. In the case of the immature creative person the inflated image he sees in his mirror would be pictured in the visual cortex (Fig. 11-B-17 and -18) and projected forward into the temporal lobe where, toward the temporal tip, it would meet two forces, one the subsidiary superego reaching it via the uncinate fasciculus (Fig. 11-D-2), the other the stream of feeling and/or libido reaching it via the caudate and amygdala (Fig. 11-A-8). If his narcissism is strong his self-love might permit him to accept this image of himself momentarily because the stream of libido from the amygdala would rationalize it; but sooner or later the punishing activity of the subsidiary superego would reject this image and he would then be overcome by guilt but unaware of its cause. In the case of the mature creative person the image reflected in his mirror would not need to be rationalized by self-love from the amygdala; the will would have been concerned not with monetary interests or biological impulses but with outer facts; its achievement could therefore have been accepted by the subsidiary superego in the temporal tip, projected back (Fig. 11-C-7) to Area 19 as a basis for activity, and thence to the pulvinar, where it could have been stored as a memory. In the case of the neurotic the debased image of himself that he sees reflected in his mirror and in the eyes of others could reach his visual cortex and from there be projected toward the temporal tip, where it would be further affected by the punishing activity of his immature maternal superego. Outer reality would thus seem to confirm what he already knows, that he is inferior. The resulting psychic product would be projected back to Area 19, where it would serve as a basis for his activity, and to the pulvinar, where it would serve as a memory. In this case, then, the individual's action would be based on the immature maternal superego and the resulting primitive and infantile conscious will, on its debased image in the inner projection field (Area 24), and on the *actual* image established in the pulvinar and Area 19 from the outer world. These actions would seem to conform with both the inner and the outer facts; but the individual would be entirely inadequate to take his part in normal activity and would suffer continually from a painful feeling of inferiority.

It now becomes evident that the harmonious relationship of the average, well-adjusted person to the world of other persons about him depends in part on the operation of his perceptual faculties, which are here placed in the temporal lobe. He projects the image of himself onto the other persons of his group, who have more or less similar wills and superegos, i.e., similar

moral standards, and in turn receives and identifies with an approving reflection of himself in their eyes. This reflection is the major element in the
development of his superego and his moral standards. For his superego is
not an individual development, as in the strong-willed creative individual,
but a part of the collective superego of his group. This fact makes for greater
happiness on his part but also tends to maintain the status quo and to shut
out the creative individual, without whose activities we all might still be
living in caves.

The mechanisms of the temporal lobe postulated here, with their explanation of the action of the perceptual faculties, thus provides an understanding
of identification, which plays such an important role in psychotherapy. For
the neurotic with his strong opposing will but immature superego and
primitive conscious will perceives in the therapist an authority who evidently
has a strong basis for self-restraint, self-confidence, and moral decisions, but
who does not exhort. Since these are the qualities for which he hungers,
and usually has the capacity to develop, and since his opposing will is not
aroused to opposition by exhortation, he is generally quite ready to reach
out toward what he wants from the therapist. In this process of reaching
out he projects his real biological self, in its immature form, onto the therapist, while relying on the therapist's restraint to prevent an answering
response to his projected libido. In this way he is leaning on the superego
of the therapist during this developmental period, taking it in through his
perceptual faculties (in the temporal lobe) and establishing it as his subsidiary superego (at its tip) until, at the termination of the therapy, he has
established his own superego in his own ego structure and can altogether
discard the therapist.

Dreamy states.—With this understanding of temporal lobe function it
is now possible to consider the dreamy states already mentioned. We may
first select for discussion the case of a woman who died of a tumor of the
temporal tip.[77] This patient was a very fat, widowed cook of fifty-three seen
in November and December, 1887, the last two months before she died,
with paresis of her left side and bilateral optic neuritis. Her seizures began
thirteen months before with tremor of the hands and arms and the apparition
of an agreeable, silent, little black woman actively engaged in cooking. The
patient would stand with her eyes fixed straight ahead for a few moments
and then say "what a horrible smell"; she turned a leaden color, had a suffo-
cating feeling, and passed her urine, but remembered everything during the
seizure; she did not struggle or bite her tongue and never believed the specter
to be a real person; when she had to give up cooking the seizures continued
with the sense of smell, but without the apparition. In the hospital she was

---

[77] John Hughlings Jackson, *Selected Writings* (2 vols.; London: Hodder and
Stoughton, Ltd., 1932) I, 406.

found to have a normal sense of smell, taste, and hearing; she sometimes had the delusion that she had got up and walked, or complained in an aggrieved way that she had tried to get up and been flung back in bed, i.e., projected her disability onto an outside source; but she gradually became more torpid physically and mentally, developed a left hemiparesis and a bilateral optic neuritis, and died at the end of December. Section of the brain revealed a small, round-celled sarcoma the size of a tangerine involving the extreme tip of the right temporal lobe and especially that part of it anterior to the uncus of the hippocampal gyrus, which contains the amygdala; the growth compressed the lenticular nucleus and the internal capsule and so accounted for the paralysis. The tumor thus involved the two portions of the temporal tip previously postulated to modify the incoming data from the outer world, i.e., the subsidiary superego and the amygdala, but it also involved the prepyriform area which receives the stimuli from the olfactory bulb. This latter involvement must have stimulated the sense of smell nonspecifically, but the remainder of the attack might be conceived to result from partial destruction of the other two structures in the temporal tip, which, according to our theory, regulate the organization of the incoming data into a psychic product which accords with the individual's previous estimate of the reality of the outer world.

Now the patient's apparition was evidently the result of a fantasy in which she represented herself as busily engaged in her usual occupation in a kitchen. The person thus seen was agreeable but black; this blackness may represent self-derogation in connection with the facts that she had to cook with coal (kitchens were often in cellars) and that at that time in England servants sometimes referred to themselves as "creatures"—they had a permanent sense of inferiority to the upper classes; the horrible smell might have been her interpretation of impending disaster connected with her tumor and projected to the area receptive to odors and stimulated by it, the prepyriform lobe. It is noteworthy, too, that the horrible smell was connected with a *sense of suffocation*, for the temporal tip, like the orbital surface, projects to both the respiratory and vasomotor centers,[78] and this projection to the medulla may have caused her to pass her urine, though the paths by which this could occur are not clear. No evidence is given that she had not previously had other fantasies of a different nature and she would normally have withheld this secret information; the record does not state explicitly whether the attacks occurred when she was alone or with other people. But the agreeableness of the little black woman is evidently self-approval. She was then ambivalent toward herself. This fantasy might have been projected into Area 24-23, from there to Areas 18 and 19, with which it associates (Fig. 11-B-9),[79] and then into the temporal lobe where it would have

[78] Fulton, *Phys. N.S.*, p. 363.   [79] Brodal, *op. cit.*, p. 208.

been *in part* evaluated as real because of partial destruction of the subsidiary superego. In this roundabout way, the fantasy would momentarily have taken on enough of the aspects of reality to permit the seizure, which was labeled epileptic though she had no convulsion. If this person's psyche could be studied now it might be found that she was a strong-willed person who often had fantasies of another nature. For example, strong-willed persons after awakening in the morning and while still lying abed often have sexual fantasies connecting them with another person in a relationship which gives them erotic feelings and takes on all the aspects of reality until they arise and turn on the light; this action suddenly brings them back to reality and shatters the illusion, possibly because it produces activity of the temporal tip which destroys the illusion of reality produced by projecting the fantasy from Area 23 to Area 19 (Fig. 11-B-9) and from there into the temporal lobe.

Psychical seizures.—But other cases with somewhat similar temporal lobe seizures have been studied by more modern methods.[80] These were persons who had hallucinations and focal cerebral seizures diagnosed by electroencephalographic methods as arising in the temporal lobe. Each was sufficiently incapacitated to suggest that an organic lesion might exist in the temporal lobe and each was operated upon under local anesthesia, an osteo-plastic flap being turned back so as to expose a large portion of the pre- and postcentral gyri and of the parietal and temporal lobes; the exposed brain surface was then stimulated by electrodes and an electroencephalographic record often taken from the neighboring cortex. In some cases a tumor or adhesions were found but in others the records do not indicate that any lesion was found, though the electroencephalograph showed that "spikes" arose in the temporal lobe.

The first case to be cited here[81] is that of a girl of fourteen who for three years had had epileptiform seizures, sometimes with general convulsions, and whose brain, on exposure under local anesthesia, showed adhesions between the dura and arachnoidea and atrophy of the (temporal?) convolutions, most marked posteriorly. In infancy, after an anesthetic, she had a single convulsion followed by coma and transient hemiplegia. At the age of seven while walking in a field with her brothers a man came up behind her and said, "How would you like to get into this bag with the snakes?" Badly frightened and screaming she ran home with her brothers to relate the event to the mother; the brothers recalled the event and the man; the mother remembered the fright and the story. There followed an occasional nightmare re-enacting the scene until at the age of eleven she began to have seizures. These were characterized by sudden fright, screaming, and recall of the cir-

---

[80] Penfield and Rasmussen, *op. cit.*, p. 157.
[81] *Ibid.*, p. 164.

cumstances of her terror at the event experienced at the age of seven. During the attack she was conscious of her environment and able to call persons about her by name, but so possessed by the terror in her hallucination, and by fear lest she be struck from behind and smothered, that she seemed to be two persons at the same time. After admission to the hospital a seizure was reproduced by hydration and withdrawal of medication.

Stimulation of the cortex at points posteriorly near the visual cortex reproduced in the patient the visual parts of her hallucinations, stimulation at points further forward in the secondary auditory cortex reproduced the auditory parts, together with dread, and at the most anterior points she reacted by saying, "They are yelling at me for doing something wrong." This sequence is significant.

This was an operation which she hoped would cure her frightening attacks and naturally she would be alerted for the memories of the original event with its terrifying sequelae; she was an adolescent whose will was still undeveloped because of its domination by her immature maternal superego and who therefore would be fearful and feel guilty under many circumstances. In her waking periods her superego must have suppressed this painful memory as far as possible, just as it suppressed sadistic expression of the opposing will; and the greater the suppression the more likely it would be for the will to recall it. In her sleep, when the incoming stream of impulses from the outer world had ceased to flow, the following might be supposed to occur: her timid will would be emboldened to recall the memory here supposed to be stored away in the pulvinar, to project it to Area 24-23 where it would become conscious as a dream, and from there to Area 19 and the temporal lobe where, like normal incoming visual stimuli, it would assume the aura of reality. If this patient had had no demonstrable pathology the frightening dream might have recurred and awakened her from time to time as a compulsion resulting from a punishing superego. The sequence of the different stimulations while the brain was exposed during the operation would be significant because it traced the path which the memory would have had to take to have such verisimilitude, until, as it approached the subsidiary superego at the temporal tip, first dread and then guilt were evoked. One might suppose, then, that this path had become sensitized by the pathology described in this patient but that the attachment of this particular memory to it was purely coincidental and had its origin in the patient's psyche, that the memory of it was therefore not stored in the temporal lobe.

The view just expressed, that the attachment of the dream content to the lesion is purely coincidental, is supported by the next succeeding case in the series of psychical epileptiform seizures,[82] a pastor of twenty-seven in

[82] *Ibid.*, p. 167.

whose temporal lobe a tumor was found but without any very definite repro-
duction of the dream on stimulation of the cortex by electrodes; after removal
of the tumor and roentgen therapy, the attacks came at longer intervals but
the *dream content altered* from time to time.

The third case in this series was again a girl of fourteen whose major
seizures were inaugurated by an aura in which she seemed to be in a park
where she usually saw a boy but once a girl. Operation was suggested because a superficial electrographic focus was demonstrated in the right temporal lobe. Exposure of the brain revealed no demonstrable lesion, according
to the record, but at most points stimulation produced some portion of the
dream and at one point she thought one of the persons in the dream was her
mother. This patient was an adolescent girl and her hallucination of seeing
a boy in the park and having a "sick feeling" in her throat at the same time
suggests to one familiar with dreams and with Rank's psychology that she
had denied the male genitalia and therefore had to identify with the male.
According to our hypothesis this might result in projection of her own
image as a boy to Area 24-23 and then to Area 19 and the temporal lobe;
there it would take on verisimilitude and come into conflict with the subsidiary
superego representing the immature maternal superego. This conflict is suggested by the "sick feeling" in the throat (projection to the medulla?) and
by the fact that at one point stimulated she saw the mother, who represents
the superego, among a lot of other people.

The absence of any lesion except the superficial electrographic temporal
focus suggests the possibility that this focus might have resulted from such
a conflict alone. This hypothesis would explain the epileptiform attacks in
some of the subsequent cases without organic lesions in this series of psychical
seizures. In other words it seems possible that a will conflict of such elemental importance as to involve libido and the determination of the individual's sexual activities might by constant repetition cause an electrographic
focus when projected to the temporal lobe by a strong-willed person. For
it is in the strong-willed person that such conflicts occur and it is they in
whom the will attempts to realize itself; the paths by which this realization
might take place in the temporal lobe have been pointed out. In this connection it should be remembered that libido and/or feeling have been postulated
to arise in the hippocampus and that this has been shown to present pathological lesions in epileptics.

It is now of interest to consider the interesting experimental work of
Klüver, who extensively removed the hippocampus, uncus, and amygdala
in addition to most of the temporal neocortex on both sides in monkeys.[83]
If the present writer's conception of temporal lobe function is even approxi-

---

[83] Heinrich Klüver, "Brain Mechanisms and Behavior with Special Reference to
the Rhinencephalon," *Journal-Lancet*, CXXII, No. 12 (December 1952), 567.

mately correct Klüver's operation would (1) interrupt the cortical circuit for libido (hippocampus → fornix → mammillary body → anterior thalamic nuclei → cingular gyrus → cingulum → hippocampus), (2) remove the subsidiary superego which, by arousing fear, protects the monkey against danger from outside sources such as snakes (of which the monkey is terrified), (3) remove the amygdala, which permits the monkey to project its libido onto other monkeys, and (4) remove the path by which objects in the outer world are projected back to Area 19 and thence to the personality in the prefrontal lobe by way of the inferior occipitofrontal fasciculus. In other words, while in no sense blind, the monkey in its relation to the outer world would be seriously disturbed, the mechanism by which it projected its feeling onto others would be absent, its sexuality would find no outlet, and it might then regress to an infantile stage. Many (but not all) of the behavior symptoms in Klüver's operated monkeys would thus be satisfactorily explained.

Summary

A theory of temporal lobe function based on known anatomic facts and connections, on associations demonstrated by strychnine studies, and on the will psychology of Otto Rank has been devised. This theory explains the temporal lobe as the site of integration of data from the outer world (outer reality) into a psychic product which we may call the "object." This object would be subjected to two psychical forces—(1) a subsidiary superego at the temporal tip, and (2) libido and/or feeling in the amygdala near this tip—and so might be differently interpreted by different normal persons and misinterpreted by psychotics. The object, thus modified, would be projected to the prefrontal lobe, the site of the personality, by way of the inferior occipitofrontal fasciculus.

This conception of the function of the temporal lobe provides a mechanism which might explain the clinical phenomenon of certain cerebral seizures: narcissistic will impulses originating in the mammillary body might pass to Area 24 via the AV nucleus and thence to Area 19 where they would take on verisimilitude (see Fig. 11-B-9); from there they would pass via the inferior longitudinal fasciculus to the hippocampus and so back to the mammillary body in a kind of circus movement.

It has been indicated here that in strong-willed persons either the social self (represented here by the DM nucleus) or the biological self (represented here by the mammillary body) may predominate. The epileptic as described by Penfield is neither a neurotic nor an average person. It may be presumed that he is a strong-willed person in whom the biological self predominates and who tends therefore to solve his psychological problems outwardly rather than inwardly. This means in terms of the theories developed here that the biological self when supercharged with narcissistic feeling would tend to overpower the social self (see Fig. 1). But the superego through its connection with the social self (see Fig. 2-C) would actively resist this attempt. And since the social self is represented by the extrapyramidal system and the biological self by the pyramidal system, the conflict between them—instead of being resolved in the field of ideas, i.e., in the inner projection fields of the will (see Fig. 2-C)—would be initiated in the lateral and posterior masses of the thalamus and projected through the cortex toward the outer world, where it would be evidenced by tonic or clonic convulsions and by loss (denial) of consciousness. Since the small-celled portion of the DM nucleus is here postulated to represent the character the conflict would register here, pass thence to the prefrontal lobe and then caudad transcortically, which is precisely its path as determined electroencephalographically by Penfield.

VIII

SYNOPSIS OF TWO TREATED CASES WITH DREAMS AND THEIR INTERPRETATION

The writer believes it will clarify the problems discussed in this book to present the synopsis of two cases treated by psychotherapy. They illustrate in a practical way the projection of the will, the identification with the therapist, and the denial of feeling by the will, and reveal some of the material on which Rank constructed his genetic psychology.

By way of introduction it may be stated that patient and therapist sit facing each other informally in a living room without any of the atmosphere or paraphernalia of a physician's office. The writer feels it unwise to have the patient recline on a couch because while this may promote a tendency to fantasy it also implies submission to his rule; in fact he states implicitly that there are no rules to be followed and that the patient is free to talk about what she pleases or to keep silent when she wishes. This gives the patient a sense of freedom which is usually in marked contrast to her previous experiences, when she has often been questioned in such a way as to arouse her opposing will.

Synopsis of First Treated Case

The interpretations given here were worked out from notes taken during the course of the therapy, after consideration of all the elements that entered into each case, and in view of the end result. The patient, then, got very little of their true significance—just a few explanations from time to time to keep her projecting onto the therapist. The information that they reveal is almost entirely for him alone and if given at once would often be more hurtful than helpful to her. For the term "homosexuality" has life or death connotations to the neurotic and its casual use by the therapist is a mere gratification of his own sadismus. Her *self*-realization develops gradually as she comes to understand the early maternal relationship with its sexual implications, the relation of the nipple to the genitals, the narcissistic period, and the significance of psychological maturation with its acceptance of the adult object relationship. But she must be given no more of this than just what she needs to continue or to complete her development.

Session 1.—She is in middle life, an only child, and comes from a small California town. She complains of weakness, fatigue, and nervousness. She remembers her father as very bad-tempered and made up her mind never to allow her temper to get the best of her. She married, had a normal sex life, and was fairly contented until her husband took to drinking. Then she divorced him and supported herself. She has had a hysterectomy and no pregnancies; in fact, she never wanted a child. Her husband stopped drinking and she remarried him but has worked much of the time until she got too tired.

Session 2.—She talked about inconsequential things and then attempted to get the therapist to talk. When this failed she was silent for a time, grew quite disturbed, and began to cry; she seemed a little resentful. It was pointed out that her talk up to that time had been only to conceal her real desire, which was to cry, and that her crying was an admission of pain which was real and therefore healthy. She seemed more rested after this but said little. At the termination of the hour she appeared doubtful about coming back but when asked if she wished to do so said "yes."

In this second session the patient dropped her guard. Her opposing will had previously been suppressed by her superego and had given rise to various psychomatic complaints which made her nervous and fatigued. But the therapist accepted her opposing will by not attempting to break down her silence by questions and by not insisting that she tell all her thoughts. Her superego then relaxed somewhat. The next session shows that she began to project onto him.

Session 3.—She dreamed of a man and his wife; they owned a series of old houses made into apartments (she actually lives in one of them); the man was good-natured but not worth much; the woman was red-headed and a fine energetic worker who raised her children and attended to everything else too; in the back yard a huge hole had been dug with the dirt piled all around it; she could not climb over this dirt; a young girl of about eleven years with dimples and a sweet smile appeared; she said she liked a boy next door and he was only a year younger than she. Interpretation: the dream pictures her attitude toward man and woman with all the advantages on the woman's side; she depreciates the man. The big hole in the back yard with dirt piled about it is her way of saying these sessions are to reveal "dirt" which is to be "dug up." The dream child represents her present ideal of herself. Actually she married a man who was just the opposite of her bad-tempered father. (She was not told this.) She says her mother is sweet and lovable, likes everybody, lives near her, and has been her ideal. But it is obvious to the therapist that this is an impossible ideal for this strong-willed woman. When she was in high school she had a terrible time: she was fat, had no sex appeal and no dates. She always resented herself. Her principal did not like her and almost fought with her.

Session 4.—She dreamed she was married to a young Chinese who runs a grocery store near her and who is rather sparky about a young Chinese woman; she did not feel like going to bed with him but he said that would be all right; he did not expect it. The flat was nice and clean but there was an elevated center in the living room under the rug as though a big pipe had been built under the floor there. Interpretation: the dream shows she is projecting positively onto the therapist though she preserves her moral code and he accepts it. The elevated center under the floor possibly alludes to the phallus which she has indicated is to be kept under cover, or, like the dirt hole in a previous dream, to plumbing. In other words she now accepts the therapist as one to whom she can tell everything but the amenities are preserved. This implies that the therapist has supplanted her mother as a moral authority; i.e., she is projecting her superego onto him, telling him secrets she could never have told her mother.

She feels ever so much better, is silent and at peace most of the hour.

Session 5.—She dreamed that she was in a butcher shop to buy sausages; the butcher pulled out his genitals, put them on the table, and cut off what she wanted. Interpretation: she emasculates the therapist, i.e., makes a woman of him; his penis represents both the nipple and nourishment. She thus returns to the oral stage with the therapist as mother. She spoke of religion, could not believe it so simple as made out to be, felt that the supreme cause of everything would not be small enough to want to be worshiped. She continues to feel better.

Session 6.—She dreamed she was in a large hall; a dog lay on a table, like the coffee table in the living room where she recounted the dream; he jumped off and went to another woman in the audience. This animal played a large part in her early life. She loved it and even now cries as she talks about it; but she has previously suppressed her feeling about the animal. It grew old and feeble and finally had to be taken to the pound and killed. Interpretation: she uses the dog as a symbol for the man; it goes to another woman; she feels herself unloved. But she herself has not hitherto expressed any affection for a man though she missed her husband while they were divorced.

Dream 2: She was on a beach; there were two young hoodlums who were breaking bottles of milk on porches; she reproved them and they took after her; then they were in a boat taking after her and as they approached the boat opened its mouth and bit at her like an old cat she has. The cat actually has no teeth. Interpretation: this is not a clear dream and seems rather to deal with tendencies within herself than with her relation to the therapist. The hoodlums breaking bottles of milk might indicate her sadistic opposing will ridiculing or opposing her return to the oral stage where milk was the main food. The biting boat probably alludes to weaning for with the advent of teeth nursing usually stops. The cat has no teeth, however, and this would indicate her desire to continue nursing. The dream therefore indicates conflict between the opposing will and her primitive will. In view of her statement in Session 16, after the final date had been set, that she consciously suppressed the first upsurge of feeling toward the therapist, this dream conflict is probably connected with the suppression; i.e., the suppression impeded her progress.

Session 7.—She dreamed that she was kissing a young man she knew when she was in high school; then she was in a large hall and this man, who has since married, seized his wife and embraced her; she was embarrassed for him; he got up on a board platform above and shook down a lot of dust, to which she is allergic. Interpretation: she seems now to be leaving the oral stage and becoming adolescent; she is jealous of the woman who married her former boy friend and resentful of his shaking dust onto her. Actually she has always denied she could be jealous, obviously because she denied she could love a man—which she now admits.

She has had a tremendous upsurge of energy: came over to San Francisco to shop and is scarcely tired. She has returned to a class for exercises. She wonders whether her allergy does not develop because she hates housework.

Session 8.—She dreamed that she was in Monterey and riding in a coupé she formerly owned; she picked up a young woman; but only the parking lights would go on; the radio blared away; she stopped at a service station and an elderly attendant came out and plunged right into the radio but did not touch the light as she wanted him to do; he had a poker face and would not talk. Interpretation: the change from a male to a female companion at the adolescent period in a strong-willed woman is perhaps significant but homosexuality was not mentioned. It is quite evident that she could not continue along this line because the lights would not go on. The attendant who fussed with the radio but ignored the lights is evidently the therapist. In other words she projected her superego onto him. She seems very subdued.

Session 9.—She is full of good spirits again. She dreamed she had come here in a car and her husband waited outside for her. There was a young man with hands like claws; he clutched at her and tried to drag her upstairs; she awoke in terror. Interpretation: the therapist gesticulates often with his hands; the young man was evidently meant to represent him. She is projecting her sexual impulses onto him, making him the guilty party, but the fact that she has her husband outside and that she awoke in terror shows her guilt feeling. Her will is now conscious and freely expressed, her superego directly opposed to it.

Session 10.—She was very much shocked by the facts revealed in last week's dream and is still getting over it. She did not like the idea that she might have had this sort of feeling for other men all these years without knowing it. She had a real sexual problem before marriage as her libido was strong. She solved it by keeping company with her boy friends only a short time and then leaving them. At last she found a man she felt she could marry, her husband. Her sex life, she says, has been full and satisfactory with him.

Evidently her will reacted against the restraints taken on by identification with her mother and this must have contributed somewhat to her strong sexual desire.

Session 11.—She has felt bad all this week and thinks it may be due to the fact that acacia is in bloom; but she is not sure that it is not due to psychological difficulty. She now seems quite friendly. She dreamed that she was working for a physician (the therapist's son). Her office was down the hall and she found it difficult to go down to the reception room to watch the patients and back to her office. Interpretation: She herself puts an obstacle in her path to show that her progress is slow and difficult.

Dream 2: She dreamed that a couple came to visit them and when the man could find no place to sit she said in a friendly way: "Come sit in my lap." Interpretation: this shows the beginning transformation of libido into friendly feeling?

Dream 3: She dreamed that she went to a butcher shop but did not like the long piece of meat the man put out; it fell to the floor but she picked it up and threw it at him; in some way it got tangled about her neck and felt cold and unpleasant. She seemed to have some squid in her hand. Interpretation: this dream must be compared with the dream in Session 3 to get its full significance. What the butcher now offers her is cold and unpleasant; she rejects it, i.e., she has left the oral stage. Probably the squid is an allegorical reference to semen or its oral counterpart, milk, but the significance of this is not quite clear; it seems to imply that at times she has relieved her husband manually.

She states that she has never wanted a baby and has always taken measures to prevent having one. She felt she never wanted to be attached to a man so closely as to bear him a child. This, of course, shows her narcissism and should be considered in relation to the woman companion in Session 8.

Session 12.—She was rather pleased last week that a strike prevented her coming and seems to enjoy telling the therapist about it. She dreamed that she was kissing her husband passionately and wanted to go to bed with him but some one came in. Interpretation: this shows she desires to abandon her narcissism and be a real wife to her husband.

Dream 2: A long-time friend got married to a suitable man. Interpretation: This probably means her change in relation to her husband.

Session 13.—She dreamed that her sister-in-law went to a shower for her daughter. She generally looks dowdy and her religion forbids lipstick but this time she was all tidied up and looked quite smart; but she had not used lipstick. Interpretation: This probably means her acceptance of womanly traits but she maintains her spiritual, i.e., religious, values.

Dream 2: She dreamed that she had been to some kind of a parade and someone gave her what she was told was her car to drive home; she got into rough country and found the going tough with brush obstructing the road. She came to a family of Okies; there was a naked child of about two with stringy hair to her shoulders and a repulsive old man, also naked. She was afraid the child would get in the way of the car and grew irritated. Then she found the car was not hers but instead an old wreck. Interpretation: This is very significant. She wants to leave the therapist—the parade is over. The car he has provided is a wreck. The going is to be tough. He is repulsive and naked, i.e., sexual in his interpretations. The child (which she conceived for him) is unattractive and in her way.

She now feels that things have come to a stop. When this statement is considered in relation to the dream child it shows that the final date should be set. She is to have only twelve more sessions.

The appearance of a child usually is a symbol of rebirth but this child presages difficulties to come (see Addendum).

Finale

Session 14.—She dreamed but forgot completely the details. She remembers only that she was like a man. She sometimes looks in the glass and hates seeing her eyes because they are like her father's. He never showed feeling for anybody. This dream fragment and her consequent statements show that her present conflict is between her sadistic opposing will and her undifferentiated libido. She has never wished to admit feeling for a man, nor has she wanted to be mother to a child. She has thus denied a woman's two main functions. She is quite silent and seems rather hard.

This illustrates the statements made earlier in this book that libido can remain crude and undifferentiated and be unaccompanied by real feeling. In this case her sexual response was normal: the libido was projected to the labia and vagina. Her guilt then arose because the crude undifferentiated libido easily became attached to another man and had to be rejected by her superego. This necessary denial of libido by the opposing will caused her fatigue and nervousness.

Session 15.—She has been tired and has felt bad since last week; cannot see what the trouble it. She dreamed that she was younger and unmarried. She was in some kind of a guest house where everyone was quite friendly. The handsome young man in the next room was one she had been engaged to but had turned down for her present husband. He had a large veal loaf and wanted her to go out with him to the place he had bought it so he could pay for it. She had on only her shorts and a morning coat but went along to the country store. He went in and seemed to take a long time. Her present husband appeared and she kissed him and explained that she was waiting for the other man. Then she was out behind the store; there was a lovely stream with shaded nooks and water animals like turtles; a snake appeared and swam around with his head standing up.

She then asked if the snake was not a sexual symbol. Interpretation: Her undifferentiated libido easily attaches itself to another man. Her idyllic description of the country stream shows how easy it is to rationalize libido. But her husband is in the background. There is still conflict between the libido and her superego. She says she loves her husband and is in tears; she does not like the part of herself she has discovered: it is selfish just like her father.

Dream 2: Someone was getting married and she went upstairs to get dressed; when she finished she found the wedding was over. Interpretation: This seems to indicate remorse; she missed a real marriage.

Session 16.—She is in tears and exhausted from unpleasant thoughts racing through her head. Some of this is fear of homosexuality, she says. She thinks this might have been a possibility in adolescence. She dreamed that she was with several women who were going bathing; she was menstruating, planned to swim in her underwear and was looking for a place to discard her pad; she entered a place where a man was working and he asked what she wanted; she said she was looking for a rest room; he said this was a men's room but it would be all right for her to use it; she said she could not do that. Interpretation: She is now in the so-called Oedipus stage of development; her narcissism makes her tend toward the woman (a replica of herself); this would make her masculine, but her superego makes her reject this.

Dream 2: A married friend and her husband were in her home; the woman had gone out and the man was to follow; a button was loose on his coat and the patient hastened to sew it on for him. Interpretation: Friendly feeling is developing out of libido.

Dream 3: She dreamed that a woman friend was with her and had put some pencil at the corner of her eyes but had turned it down. She told her friend that the pencil should turn up, not down. Interpretation: The tendency of upturned lines at the corner of the mouth and eye is to indicate good will, a downturned line to indicate ill will.

She is cheered up by the interpretations but is still disconsolate and afraid she will not be able to resolve her conflict. She states that when she first had an upsurge of feeling toward the therapist she was afraid of it and consciously suppressed it.

Session 17.—She looks and feels much better; there is more expression in her face. She has been frightfully tired and has slept a great deal. She dreamed that she went to a stylish French restaurant; they decided to order roast beef though it was very high, $6.35 a plate; the receptionist came along with a guerney; they put her on it and took her for an electrocardiogram. Interpretation: This probably referred to last week's session when she felt so bad and the price therefore seemed too high; in fact she felt so bad she could hardly get up the stairs and so thought that an electrocardiogram was indicated.

Dream 2: She dreamed she was kissing her husband passionately and was standing on a slippery place but did not fall. Interpretation: She shows feeling and libido toward her man but the ground is still uncertain. This is in marked contrast to the dream where two men were in the picture.

Dream 3: She dreamed she was in a dentist's office because of an abscessed tooth; but he said the tooth did not have to come out, that the process would resolve itself. Interpretation: This goes back again to the weaning period; the tooth does not have to come out, i.e., she cannot continue with oral nourishment.

Dream 4: She dreamed of a high toilet onto which she had to get up to urinate. She has often dreamed of dirty toilets in the past. Interpretation: This refers to her toilet training, i.e., her mother's social influence; the toilet seemed high because she was small at that time. The idea of dirtiness must have come from the mother.

Session 18.—She had her husband telephone last week that she was too shaky to come over. Today she came bouncing up the stairs and said, "You see, I can go on my own power." She had a number of dreams and could hardly wait to recount them. She dreamed that a young girl and her boy friend were to get married and she helped the girl and a friend to fix up a room in an old house for them to live in; there was an old bathroom in the house but the toilet was quite clean. Interpretation: Her desire is now to put aside the mother's interpretation of the perineum as "dirty."

Dream 2: She dreamed that she was asleep and could not wake up; a salesman came to the door but her mother could not get rid of him; she herself finally got up and talked straight out to him, told him to get out; in fact, she went after him with a hot curling iron. Interpretation: She does what her mother could not do, i.e., supplants her.

Dream 3: She dreamed she was in an old house full of cobwebs; it was her old house made over into apartments; there was a very vituperous woman there who berated her but she just stood and paid very little attention to her. Interpretation: In this dream she stands up for herself to a woman, as she did in the last toward a man, i.e., she expresses her will under both circumstances.

Dream 4: She and her husband had gone up a hill after leaving their car on a road below; when they went down to get into it a woman said she had left the car with the wheels just on the rail so that when someone pushed it, it went over onto the road below; the patient stoutly maintained she had done no such thing. Interpretation: She again stands up for herself.

Dream 5: She was a receptionist in a hospital; a young woman had a baby there and the grandmother came to take the child away; but the patient called the nurse and together they put the grandmother off so the baby was kept there; he was quite cute. Interpretation: This should be compared with Dream 2 in Session 13, where the child was unattractive. She indicates now that she is "reborn" and is not going to allow her mother to influence her. The patient is full of life and animation and gestures freely; she is evidently on the road to recovery. She says she has always felt the need for integration; something prevented her from accomplishing it. Evidently it was the maternal superego which did this.

Session 19.—She dreamed that a new highway was built in front of her apartment and she had to move; the new one was not quite satisfactory since there was no kitchen; she found a Chinese restaurant downstairs where everything was quite clean. Interpretation: She is abandoning the old and taking on the new, i.e., leaving the mother-therapist on whom she has leaned. The absence of a kitchen is particularly significant when the early dreams of butchers is kept in mind; she seems a little discontented about it.

The last two days she has felt tired and did not wish to come here. She says she gets tense when she comes and the next day her legs are tired as though she had been exercising. She is quite silent but looks all right.

Session 20.—She dreamed she was talking to a friend near the levee at her old home on the river; a tall, neatly dressed, educated, and refined young man came along; her friend told her how well he was doing; then he said he had been forced to sleep alone in the warehouse at night and found it very cold. Interpretation: She is commiserating with the therapist because she is leaving him and he has to sleep alone at night; but she uses his son as a symbol for him.

Dream 2: An old-time friend she has disliked for years was sitting in a train; the patient was picking up the laundry and was supposed to give this woman a key to her home but the woman ignored her until finally a young woman sitting behind her said, "That is about all I would take"; the patient then took the woman by the shoulder and shook her heartily. Interpretation: She brings up the question of her narcissism again but has the woman ignore it and so passes it by; however, she is irritated at giving it up.

She is increasingly conscious of resentment at her mother but feels she must not show it. She feels tired all the time. As the last session approaches she brings up her old symptoms. This is an attempt to make the therapist think she is still sick and in need of more treatment than he has allowed. It was pointed out to her that before the final date was set she felt that things had come to a halt.

Session 21.—Last week on the way home in the train she sat in deep thought when an army man came in and sat just ahead of her; he had a sun-burned neck, was handsome and decorated with ribbons. She suddenly thought she would like to bite him on the neck. She laughed at this as an expression of her will that she could now accept. This shows how fully she has solved her sexual problem; she expressed it in amusing fantasy. She dreamed that her cousin came to town with her husband; she scarcely knows the man and is not sure she likes him. They were to get tickets for the light opera; then she remembered she had a laundry bill to pay and wondered if she could afford both; but she decided to go anyway. Interpretation: She hesitates momentarily about a triangle situation, her old problem, but decides she can handle it.

She feels fine this week, has no fear of coming and says she has nothing much to say. Her husband and cousin have told her how different she now is.

Session 22.—She has a friend, an older woman, she knows is frigid; there was some question of the two couples going on a picnic last week; first the friend thought she would and then again she thought she wouldn't. This got the patient in a dither. She was disturbed because she identified to some extent with this woman, became what she formerly was, i.e., was unable to maintain her will. She dreamed of an adolescent girl in shorts sitting on a window ledge in such a way as to show her genitals; she had a peculiar expression on her face. Interpretation: She again brings up the old problem of narcissism as though to show the therapist she was still not well enough to leave.

Dream 2: She was sitting on a dirty toilet; she had to be careful about her skirts because there were two men present; however, their backs were turned. Interpretation: The same bringing up of old material. She had thought herself that this was what she was doing.

She had great difficulty in getting up the slight hill approaching the therapist's house today and wipes her palms with her handkerchief continually. Coming here reminds her of her past which she would like to forget. This is all to the good; it shows she wants to get away; but bringing up old material shows she also wants to stay on, i.e., she is in conflict. This is a situation like that of her friend who first thought she would and then again thought she wouldn't. And this is why she identified with her and was disturbed.

Session 23.—She brings confused dreams of struggle. She realized last week while going home on the train that she wanted to get free and stand on her own feet but was afraid of having to do it. In support of her desire for freedom she now says she has only one session more, which is not true though the therapist said nothing about this.

Session 24.—She crawled up the stairs in tears as though half dead. She and her husband had planned to go away to the mountains over the long weekend but felt constrained to shorten the distance and go instead to the sea coast because of her mother, who is eighty-one and has high blood pressure. Reservations were made for a cottage there and she hoped he would bring her mother home and leave her there for a few days respite from the old lady. Then she remembered the high cliffs above the beach and the horrible thought of pushing her mother over the edge came to her. This thought of murder has been going through her mind ever since until she thinks she is going to lose her mind. She has been in collapse since then. She dreamed she was working for her former physician; she heard him telephone for reservations at a Hungarian restaurant where the food and wine were very good and thought he might be planning to take her out to dinner; at first the idea sounded good but then she found all his wife's things in a closet and decided he was a tricky operator she could not trust. Interpretation: She shows she has solved her old sexual problem. Her fantasy of murdering her mother shows her rejection of the old maternal restraints which have kept her from becoming free. It is interesting that she brings this up at what she had planned to be the last session as though to show the therapist she really was in desperate straits. Actually she has one more. But her distress is real enough and shows the tremendous force of this early restraint through negative identification.

It was pointed out to her that she had to solve this problem by accepting the impulse and still approving herself just as she had done with her sexual impulses.

Session 25.—She is much less disturbed than last week but still much troubled about how to handle her mother, who continually tries to baby her. But she realizes that her problem is to be firm and still not irritable with her. She dreamed she was working for a physician who had a number of small examining rooms; she found a corpse in one of them and notified the other attendants and even recent patients that they might be investigated by the police. Interpretation: This dream should be compared with the fantasy of matricide in Session 24. Now there is no guilt; indeed, the suspicion of murder is projected away onto others.

Dream 2: She stopped at a store to buy a sweater on her way to an appointment here; the time passed quickly and she began to worry lest she be late; at the appointed time she tried to phone but could not get the number and so missed her appointment. Interpretation: She created a situation whereby she missed her appointment; i.e., she really did not want to come at all.

Dream 3: An old friend who is weak and a soft touch for anyone in trouble was in a nylon nightgown and at the cab of her luxurious train; she had taken in a drunken man though they were not married. The patient felt sorry for a woman who could do this. Interpretation: This dream should be compared with that in Session 3 when the woman was elevated at the expense of the man. Now she makes the woman something to commiserate with instead of admiring her; this is evidently her old self; but she still depreciates the man, possibly only as a companion for the loose woman.

Now she has absolved herself of murder and would like to get away from the therapist. It is significant that she said nothing about future appointments or the necessity for them. In other words, she thinks she can now handle her own problems.

Discussion of First Treated Case

The foundation has previously been laid for building a theoretical ego structure from Rank's material and the writer has shown that this structure finds an almost exact anatomic counterpart. In so far as the structure of the psyche can be proved by methods presently available this anatomic counterpart supports it. But the synopsis of this case presents an opportunity to illustrate in a practical way what the forces in the psyche are, how they operate, and how this particular patient began to solve her difficult problem. In short, it provides additional evidence which supports the theories on which the structure is built.

To simplify the following discussion the terminology used will be that of the ego structure. But anatomically informed readers will readily translate this terminology into their own language with the help of Chapter VII, where the necessary facts are arranged in proper sequence.

Man's dualism.—There is evidence of this from the very beginning. For example, in Session 1 the patient's decision to restrain her temper signified a crucial suppression by the superego of negativistic expression of the opposing will which before that must have been free enough to permit its positive expression in the conscious will. The dualism is obvious again in Session 4, where she is married to the young Chinese but feels she cannot go to bed with him. Similar examples may be found throughout the synopsis.

The biological self, or primitive will.—This appears in Session 4, where she married the young Chinese, and is even more apparent in Session 5, where it is revealed as being at the oral stage.

The social self, or opposing will.—This is revealed as the force which restrains the biological self in many of the dreams.

The spiritual self, or superego.—This appears from the beginning as a force whose demands are greater than those of the environment. For example, in Session 4 her feeling that she cannot go to bed with the young Chinese shows that her superego demands submission to the social code, even though marriage to him would indicate that she should behave otherwise. Her conflict is here revealed in its entirety as one between her primitive biological self and her conscience. The attachment of this spiritual self to the mother by projection and its terrific impact on the ego is shown most dramatically in Session 24, where it is necessary for her to murder her mother in fantasy to sever this maternal restraint and so assume personal responsibility for it. That she will now be able to assume this responsibility is shown by the way in which she manages her primitive biological self in the dream of the same session. Had she not been able to cast off this maternal restraint it would have been necessary for her to regard herself as a criminal and do penance for it, so to speak, for the balance of her life. She is only able to do this by realizing that her negativistic reaction to the mother is a primitive remnant in her ego development. When she has once accepted it and paid a price in suffering (her collapse) it will gradually disappear as her ego continues its development.

Acceptance of the negative, or opposing will projections.—It is apparent in Session 2 that by "dropping her guard" is meant a significant change in her relation to the therapist. The change was that instead of unconsciously opposing him and denying this by talking about inconsequential matters she now felt free in relation to him and it came about because he accepted her negativism.

Positive or primitive will projections.—Beginning with Session 4 she projects positively onto the therapist, and usually in sexual terms. This reveals in a specific way data concerned with the earliest developmental stages but expresses these data in allegorical terms.

The change in the nature of the will expressions may easily be followed from the oral stage through the narcissistic adolescent stage in Sessions 7 and 8 when she turns from the woman (mother) to the man as object. In Session 8 it is very clear that she projects the responsibility for this (her superego) onto the therapist though he has never assumed this role. The end of these positive projections is found in Session 13, when her will reaches its full positive projection but is sadistic in character.

Nature of will more important than content.—It has previously been indicated that the nature of the will is more important than its content and can be expressed in an infinite number of ways. This is shown clearly in Session 18, Dreams 2, 3, and 4, all of which reveal that the will is now maintained regardless of circumstances or of sex.

Setting the final date.—Session 14 showed the *self*-revelation which followed this prospective finale. In other words, it showed what had been denied all these developmental years and what the patient now discovers for herself when the therapist points out her denial of feeling by the will.

The dreams that follow show that the period between setting the final date and the actual termination is one of intense struggle. In Session 24 she shows that she has finally learned to handle her sexual problem in an ethical way but has to make a last desperate effort to get rid of the maternal restraints which have so impeded her development.

Temporary lapses caused by identification with the past.—That progress is not always straightforward is shown in Session 22, when she identified with an old-time woman friend who cannot make up her mind. With this she returns to a previous level of narcissism as shown by the dream which follows. This sort of identification with persons from her past may trouble her at intervals after she leaves even though she understands at the time what she is doing.

Reinforcement of the will by a feed-back mechanism.—At two crucial periods during her treatment she was practically in collapse from "emotional stress." The first occurred in Session 16 and followed by several weeks the setting of the final date. At this time she had partly overcome her previous denial and become aware of her narcissism. Her superego was punishing her severely and thoughts of homosexuality tortured her. The second occurred between Sessions 23 and 24 when she had the fantasy of murdering her mother. On both occasions she was possessed by painful thoughts which she could not shake off; each time, the opposing will was masochistic and dominated consciousness almost completely. It was this sort of reinforcement of the will which led the present writer to the idea of a feed-back mechanism originating in the basal ganglia and described in Chapter VII.

The sado-masochistic mechanism.—This is most clearly illustrated in Session 24 when she recounted the painful collapse occurring after the fantasy of murdering her mother. The pain she suffered was a punishment inflicted by her maternal superego because of her sadistic fantasy. The relation between the self-inflicted punishment and the cruel fantasy constitutes the sado-masochistic mechanism.

It is easy to see that any person who is sufficiently self-aware to be conscious of cruel impulses may use this mechanism and then reinforce the pain further by use of the feed-back mechanism described in the previous paragraph. On such occasions these persons manifest very acute distress. This is not only evident in their state of body tension but also in the movements of their eyes. The latter continually turn from one side to the other as though seeking an avenue of escape.

The relation of the will forces to reality.—We see clearly throughout the synopsis that it is the opposing will with its attached superego that restrains the primitive will. The opposing will, then, keeps the primitive biological self in touch with reality by means of what we call guilt feeling and it does this by virtue of its visual and auditory connections with the outer world. Denial of the opposing will by the biological self is thus a denial of outer reality. The dream in Session 24 shows this clearly. For a married woman to accept a dinner invitation from a sexually inclined and married male employer would jeopardize her own standing in the community as well as that of his wife; her existence was brought to mind by *seeing* her clothes in a closet and the patient's moral problem by *hearing* him making arrangements on the telephone. These warnings thus came from the outer world which would have destroyed her standing in the community. In this sense the opposing will and superego when they function properly safeguard the individual against real danger from the outside world of other people.

On the other hand, denial of feeling and/or libido by the sadistic opposing will is also a denial of reality but in this case of the inner reality of feeling. The synopsis shows that the opposing will of this patient denied not libido but true feeling; this, too, brought about destruction, but destruction from within, i.e., self-destruction in neurosis. The history recounted in Session 1 with its recital of increasing weakness, fatigue, and nervousness shows the gradual progress of this self-destruction. The moral laws are thus shown to be an expression of physiological need; their control of the organism is almost as arbitrary as the law of gravity.

The close association of will and libido.—In the last analysis the physical symptoms derive from the identification of libido with the will. So long as this patient associated the conscious will with libido she had to deny the will because of its libidinous content. But when she allowed the libido to find on outlet in fantasy, as in the dream in Session 24, she was able to guide her actions consciously with her will and so follow the dictates of her conscience.

Integration and the ideals of maturity.—The dream in Session 3 reveals that her ideal was a childlike simplicity adapted by identification with her mother. But the subsequent revelations showed her that the integration she sought and needed not only necessitated discarding this identification (the fantasy in Session 24) and accepting the true facts of her difficult nature but struggling *toward* an ideal behavior imposed by her conscience.

Relation of the will psychology to philosophy.—It was stated in Chapter I that the two main problems of psychotherapy were identical with those of philosophy: the relation of the self to reality and the relation of the self to others in ethics. The forces which determine both of these are the opposing will with its connections to the outer world and the conscious will with its urge for physical self-satisfaction. The ethical problem is clearly illustrated in Session 4, when the patient felt she could not go to bed with the Chinese, and the relation of the self to outer reality in the way she organized the dream in Session 24. This relation of the self to reality was what concerned the great philosophers, such as Kant and Schopenhauer; they were quite aware that the phenomenon, the object as it appeared to them, might be quite different from the noumenon, the object as it really was.

Addendum

This patient returned in about a year relating that she had improved steadily until her husband's business fell off. She then took a refresher course to prepare for a half-time job. But when the time came to try for a job she got jittery again and was unable to look for one. She likes her husband but is always interested in a former beau. Her mother comes in several times every day and this makes her tense. It would be desirable to get away from her but this is impossible.

It is obvious that she still denies her feelings and that this caused the return of symptoms (jitters) when outside pressure increased. She partly suppressed them in relation to the therapist as she had in relation to her father, to her successive boy friends, and to her husband; the man was depreciated in her last dream as he was in her first. The feelings are denied by her opposing will and this makes her tense. Her ideal is that she should take a half-time job but her will is not strong enough to do it.

Two things show that she is making some progress: the first is that she is beginning to take a different attitude toward her deceased father; the second is that she says she is fonder of her husband.

She was seen twice and then told she would have to work it out alone. Not infrequently such a refusal of further treatment is necessary to make the patient accept full responsibility. Her husband telephoned the following week to say that she was often in tears at night. This expression of feeling is a good sign and indicates a lessening of her egoism.

The denial of feeling is secondary to the activity of her opposing will and its relation to her superego. The mother is a simple, well-meaning person, according to the history, so the patient cannot justify her antagonism to her. She is therefore projecting onto the mother a negativism that comes entirely from within and this constitutes her guilt. Her dreams showed that she does the same thing to the husband; in spite of a satisfactory sexual relation she has never given him real feeling. The psychotherapeutic situation gave her an opportunity to overcome this in relation to the therapist but here again the positive feeling was in part suppressed. However, since she is fully aware of what she is doing, does not blame the therapist for it, aud thus accepts full responsibility, it seems very likely that she will eventually work it out (the writer has had more than one case where full recovery did not occur until some time after the therapy had terminated, e.g., that of the stutterer mentioned earlier in this book).

In the light of her present story one thing more must be discussed. No matter how carefully the therapist avoids criticism, his interpretation of a dream inevitably invites a comparison between what is and what should be. The patient senses this and subsequent dreams may show that she is attempting to live up to what she conceives the therapist's standards to be. She does this because she has identified with him, borrowed his superego, so to speak. For example, in Dream 5, Session 18, the dream of the "cute baby" is quite evidently an attempt to correct the impression given by the dream in Session 13, where the naked child of two years had stringy hair and was unattractive. This identification is constructive and necessary and in favorable cases indicates progress. In this particular case it aided in the formation of the ideal, that she ought to get a half-time job, but as yet she is unable to live up to it. That is to say, she has not yet achieved integration as a personality.

Six months later she was seen again and on this occasion was able to admit fully her feeling for the therapist. In the light of this admission it was possible to see that it was denial of her feeling relationship to him (the mother substitute) that had prevented her full recovery. Had she been able to admit it before as she does now, the fantasy of pushing the mother object over the cliff would have been interpreted as killing off the therapist and the psychotherapeutic relationship terminated for good. This was explained to her.

She is now working half time and enjoying it but still gets very tired. Her mother remains a difficult problem but she is able now to exclude her at times by pointing out her necessity for quiet and rest. However, she is still unable to leave her at home on their weekend trips because that would make them feel too guilty. She has tried her hand at writing and gets so interested in her story that she is frightened lest she be unable to get back to reality. This shows her need to express her strong will in fantasy and on a make-believe plane.

Synopsis of Second Treated Case

This case presents a different type of problem, namely that of a woman who, though married, was unable to achieve the orgasm in normal intercourse. Her husband had therefore to titillate her clitoris to give her sexual satisfaction. This showed that she was still in the narcissistic stage. Her husband appears from her statements to have been equally disturbed in his development, which justified a statement made earlier in this book, that one neurotic usually marries another.

Session 1.—This patient, a thirty-three-year-old typist and receptionist, had some psychological discussions with the therapist eight years ago, just after her marriage. She seemed satisfied at the time but her present story shows that the result was entirely unsatisfactory for it now appears that the libido remained attached to the clitoris. Her husband purchased a few acres in a neighboring county and expected her to take care of some chickens and rabbits. She hated this life and hoped she would get sick so as to escape from it; ulcerative colitis was the result. Meanwhile she bore a child who is now four. Treatment of the colitis did not help her and two years ago she again applied to the therapist for help; she was put into other hands at once and sent to a hospital where she got rapidly worse. An iliostomy and finally a colectomy were resorted to; now she has no colon and no symptoms but has to wear a bag. Her husband applied for a divorce; she was given the child, some alimony for two years, and an allowance for care of the child after that. The husband has been taking some group psychotherapy; he has visited her since the divorce and had sex relations with her; he likes to rub his penis over her breasts and asks her to take it in her mouth. She has done this at times but with great loathing and a very guilty feeling; she feels she is not strong enough to resist his demands.

She is in tears and inclines to blame herself for everything. Her father was a "bum" and she hated him; her mother is in a state institution for the insane. She and her two brothers were raised in a Jewish orphan home; as a child she was rebellious and was often told she was "bad." She left the institution at eighteen to take a job and has always been able to take care of herself since. She now wants psychological help.

Session 2.—Dream 1: She dreamed that a woman of about fifty whom she knows and likes telephoned her. Interpretation: The dream shows that the patient denies her own will by putting the responsibility for the telephone call onto this woman; she probably represents the therapist and makes a mother of him at once; not only that, but this establishes him as one to whom she can confess the most intimate things, i.e., as her superego.

Dream 2: She was out with a man who felt sexually inclined toward her; he took her into a toilet and had intercourse with her but the emission was of urine instead of semen. She dreaded to tell the therapist this dream because she felt guilty about it; she feels generally antagonistic toward men. In association with this dream she remembers that at three and a half years a boy of sixteen took her into a toilet and made her watch him urinate. Interpretation: This is a wholly narcissistic dream in which she plays both roles. The passive one she takes herself as she does in relation to her husband's amorous and aberrant advances; the active masculine one must be attributed to her biological self and reveals the origin of her neurosis; this one she projects onto the therapist. In this connection it must be remembered that she has a younger brother whose development was also disturbed, as will be shown in material presented later. She denied his genitalia and his existence and therefore had to identify with him; this established a second and a masculine-like superego which was in conflict with her own (on the opposite side); and this allowed her to play the two different roles. The alternative is identification with the sixteen-year-old boy but the sibling seems the more likely one. Her guilt is now understandable because it arises within herself but is projected onto another in the dream. Very little of this interpretation was given to the patient.

Session 3.—Dream 1: Her older brother and his wife, who are happily married, got divorced and then married people who were just the opposite of themselves, he to a very quiet, uninteresting woman and she, who detests movies, to someone who liked them. Interpretation: The significance of this dream is not entirely clear. But the divorce suggests her own situation and the remarriage her relationship with the therapist. Since she played a double role in Session 2 it may be that she does the same thing here: in her masculine role she finds her feminine self uninteresting; in her feminine role she detests what her masculine self likes.

Dream 2: She was a young girl and went out hunting monkeys with two other girls from the children's home; they shot three monkeys; when they got home the other girls were each rewarded by the housemother with a dress, but she got nothing and was furious. Interpretation: Monkeys have long tails and the term "tail" is often applied to the phallus. In this sense each girl has what serves during the narcissistic period as a "tail," i.e., a clitoris; three monkeys were shot, one for each girl; but each of the other girls was rewarded with a dress, a badge of femininity, while she alone got none and therefore remained masculine; she is furious because she is not really a woman yet.

She spent the balance of the hour telling the therapist how cruel her husband had been to her; i.e., she projected negatively onto the man.

Session 4.—She dreamed that a psychologist, a woman she formerly knew, married a man younger than she but had intercourse with him before marriage; i.e., the psychotherapeutic situation now becomes libidinous. Here for the first time she creates a libidinous situation directly involving both herself and the therapist though the sex roles are reversed. This seems like progress when compared with the almost completely narcissistic dreams that have preceded it.

She feels she is getting over her feeling of guilt about the man (her masculine identification) and that she and her ex-husband are now more friendly; her speech is somewhat clearer; she speaks up for herself better. These changes are undoubtedly due to the freer expression of her opposing will in regard to her husband, i.e., telling the therapist how cruel the husband had been.

Session 5.—She brought such incomplete fragments of three dreams that nothing could be made of them; she was talking to cover up her desire to keep silent and this was explained to her; then she broke down in tears and told the therapist she had unaccountably done the same thing at the office where she works. During her crying spell she explained how terrible it was in the hospital to have everyone come in and examine her like a curiosity. She said her former husband was sensitive about being Jewish; she herself is proud of it. Her pain seems to be self-punishment resulting from the free expression of her opposing will, which is now turned in against her ego instead of out toward her husband (the sadomasochistic mechanism).

Session 6.—Her ex-husband came to see her last week and made sexual overtures to her but she was able to handle him so diplomatically that he desisted. Then she dreamed they were married again. Yesterday she was out driving with her brother and an older man who told her that if he were younger he would go for her; she thought he ought to save such feelings for his wife. That night she dreamed that a young, attractive man was interested in her sexually though he is married; later she had an orgasm. Interpretation: She now projects her libido onto a *man* who is suitable except that he is married. This shows improvement, though her will is still sadistic because she chooses a married man.

She seems fearful about sex as though it were still connected with a person of the same sex. But she is much more cheerful and approves herself more. She says she has a rather strict code about sex and feels sad that most men approach women that way even when they are married.

Session 7.—She dreamed that she was warm and comfortable in bed but it was cold and snow was falling; the large, flat flakes did not melt when they fell to the ground. Interpretation: She is more self-contained, dignified, and is indifferent to the atmosphere at these sessions which she now seems to feel is chilly (the therapist does not project onto her).

She is getting along better with her job and says she notices in her associates some of the traits she is getting over (she is probably projecting her former difficulties onto them).

Session 8.—She dreamed that her brother and sister-in-law got a divorce. Interpretation: In view of the dream in Session 7 and of what follows, this seems to indicate that she desires to leave the therapist. She is showing a distinct and healthy feeling of resistance to him, in marked contrast to what she showed at first; but tears came to her eyes when she admitted it. She has thoughts of quitting her job (another sign of growing independence) and getting a job as executive secretary but doubts whether she can fill it properly (suspicion that she is overestimating her ability, i.e., suspicion that she is denying). She is now expressing her will to be free and independent and the final date should soon be set.

Session 9.—There were no dreams. She had a minor row with one of her women bosses but it turned out all right: she stood up for herself. She shows growing independence, is talking more distinctly, and notices this herself. She went to a dance with a girl friend and had all the dances she wanted; this was in marked contrast to a former occasion when she felt inferior and had no dances. She finds she likes her ex-husband better than many other men she meets but then tears come into her eyes and she thinks this may be silly. The final date was then set so as to allow her sixteen sessions more; this will give her a total of twenty-five.

Finale

Session 10.—Dream 1: She met a woman she had known on the street; the woman stopped to speak to her but she coolly passed her up. Interpretation: She now ignores the woman, i.e., is no longer masculine, but this somewhat sadistic attempt to deny her former self presages difficulties to follow.

Dream 2: She was in a room with other people; the therapist came to the door naked but holding a towel over his middle; the patient asked him to come in and get warm; he answered that he was plenty warm. Interpretation: She is indifferent to the naked and therefore sexually inclined therapist and so imputes her own sexuality to him (he is plenty warm).

She seems quite self-confident, is taking a course in public speaking. A man she met at a dance asked her to go out a couple of times, once to go fishing; she was able to handle him all right. She wonders what she will do to establish a relationship with a man once she has left here; she is speaking much more distinctly.

Session 11.—She has quit her job and is going to look for something better, possibly an executive job. She is quite critical of the man who is taking her out and seems to think he is not interesting enough.

Session 12.—This is the last day of her present job and she felt so confident she went out and bought herself a new suit; previously she had worn clothes given her by friends. She appears now in a red sweater and bright-colored scarf. In her class for public speaking she got up to tell a funny story.

Session 13.—At her public speaking class last night she got up to talk and became so frightened she had to sit down; but later she was able to get up again and talk. Her family have scolded her for leaving her job; she is appalled and frightened by her failure at class and breaks down in tears. The final date for separation from the mother-therapist was set in Session 9 and only now is she getting its full import. The delay shows the strength of her sadistic denial of the feeling she has for maternal support and the fear connected with losing it. After her class last night she dreamed she was the only one of a large group who got a prize for spelling. Interpretation: Self-consolation.

Session 14.—She had had a ghastly week and has been unable to go downtown to look for work. Dream 1: She had gone to an older woman to tell her that she and her ex-husband were going to be married again; this woman became enveloped in a white mist and disappeared, leaving a baby in her place; or was it a little dog? She could not tell which. Interpretation: The travail of the past week results in a *miraculous* rebirth but her doubt as to whether the creature was really human shows her uncertainty about herself.

Dream 2: She felt libido and was aware of a phallus but had no orgasm. In association with this dream she states that her younger brother took after her once and would have violated her had she permitted it. Interpretation: This may represent overcoming of her denial of the penis and the incident associating her younger brother seems to connect the denial with him. She states that a couple of years before her marriage she went with a young man and they both liked to "pet"; this was not the case with her ex-husband.

Session 15.—Dream 1: She was joining the army and going away. Interpretation: A typical dream of separation.

Dream 2: There was some question of remarriage to her ex-husband but he was already married and had two children; there was a volcano with smoke pouring out, also a big barge with many people caught in a whirlpool and flood. Interpretation: Return to her former married status is now impossible; she is now separated from the therapist; her world has ended in fire and flood.

She has done a lot of sewing but has been unable to go downtown to look for work; she is fearful and feels very much alone; there seems to be a void within her, she says. The reality of her feeling now completely overcomes her sadismus.

Session 16.—She says today she could scarcely sit through the last session. Dream 1: She was dressed in yellow and one of many others dressed in white on a great truck; there were many white flowers and someone put some in her hand; they turned out to be handkerchiefs. Interpretation: She is separated from others by a yellow Jewish gaberdine and in mourning for that part of herself she has lost (flowers in her hand which turn out to be handkerchiefs to wipe away her tears).

Dream 2: Two men lay naked on a bier; the one beneath was dead, the other moribund, and someone was attempting to revive him with an injection; the needle had a curved point like the end of a penis. Interpretation: The lower man represents her male identification, the other her ex-husband, whose sexual love she would like to revive.

Dream 3: She was much younger and thinner and some man was fondling her all over. Interpretation: She is now projecting her libido onto a man again, i.e., overcoming her denial.

Though feeling very frightened she has talked better and gone to her class, where she was able to get up and speak. She notices now that she is not so liable to look at the fly of men's pants as she always did before. This shows that denial of the genitalia causes the compulsion to look at them. She also notices that she is more willing to cook for herself and wash her dishes instead of going out for a hamburger. She looks very much sobered and is thinking of looking for work.

Session 17.—Though she still feels very bad she laughs a lot more at this session and on two occasions has gone downtown to look for work. She has dreamed vaguely about death.

Session 18.—She dreamed that she was talking to a man; there were a lot of small children dressed only in shirts, i.e., without pants; they were all girls but one. Interpretation: She no longer denies the phallus or her discarded self.

Other persons have remarked that she laughs much more. She has had a temporary job, is firmer with her child during the weekends when he is at home; and he reacts well to this. She was able to stand up easily in class and say a few words; she is able now to appreciate the difference between will and libido.

Session 19.—She has worked for three days of the past week and no longer talks of distress. She remembers one dream fragment in which she had gray hair (as a result of what she has gone through). In this connection she says that none of the terrible experiences with her ulcerative colitis and her operation were as bad as the torture of the last few weeks since the setting of the final date. When her ex-husband brought their child to her apartment this week, he was late and they both got provoked at each other; she was disturbed by this for some hours afterward. It is common for these patients to identify with their past, i.e., to revert to their old self for a time in the presence of someone out of this past. Her rectal wound has now healed and she no longer has to wear a pad.

Session 20.—Dream 1: She was walking in a wood with a child and an older woman (but not an old woman); they came to a clearing where there were cultivated flowers; the older woman picked some of them and she did not like it.

Ordinarily she likes to pick flowers and have them in her house. Interpretation: She plays both roles, the older, more mature woman is her present self (the gray hair in Session 19) who takes a common-sense attitude toward nature and uses sophistication (the cultivated flowers) for decoration; the younger woman is her former immature self and is irritated because she would have liked to leave things as they were, unsophisticated.

Dream 2: She was watching her guppy female bear her young ones though the event was not expected for some time. Interpretation: She now faces the genitals and the natural events connected with them instead of denying them.

She is extraordinarily improved and passed a physical examination for a permanent job in spite of her colectomy. She talks about almost everything except her troubles, which means she thinks she has none. Her child improves in attitude as she improves.

Session 21.—She saw her ex-husband last Saturday and dreamed the following two nights. Dream 1 : Young women were lying down with their heads in each other's laps ; her ex-husband kissed one of them. Interpretation : This dream is definitely connected with seeing her ex-husband and identifying with her old self (homosexuality) ; it shows him as interested in her former self and therefore disturbed in *his* development.

Dream 2 : Her ex-husband was showing her his penis and it was flaccid ; she did not feel sexually aroused either. Interpretation : This seems to indicate that with her psychological maturation they are no longer interested in each other sexually, or that she is no longer autoerotic.

She is not impressed with her new job; she saw her older brother and felt irritated for a moment but then realized that she could control this "sadismus" and maintain herself now. She is making conversation and really has little to say.

Session 22.—She is slightly depressed but dreamed that someone told her she had pretty eyes and a lovely complexion. Interpretation : one sees clearly how fear is covered by libido though this is projected (imputed) to another. It is noteworthy that the libido is now in the form of feeling.

Session 23.—She has had dreams all this week but remembers only one: she was on a beach under a big tree (the wisdom tree?) ; a swarm of bees were after her; by a tremendous effort she was able to get a double blanket over her so as to avoid all but a few stings; then she was walking on the water. Interpretation : The swarm of bees and their stings represent part of her old self whose impulses still annoy her though she can now protect herself from the pain of their stings by a tremendous effort ;[1] her walking on the water represents her victory (but this victory seems almost too good to be true).

She allowed her ex-husband to kiss her once this week but there was no libido in it. Once during the week she was disturbed because she had sexual thoughts in connection with a young widower but then again she realized that there was no feeling of libido in connection with it and the next day was able to see him without any such thoughts. In other words, the remnants of her primitive will are still operative but the libido is now more under control (no autoeroticism).

Session 24.—She dreamed that she had an orgasm from masturbating but remembers that it was connected with the labia and not the clitoris; she thinks she did this to prove to herself that she was a woman.

[1] A tree is often a symbol for the phallus and the swarm of bees might be interpreted as spermatazoa; but these interpretations would be out of context.

She talks a good deal about her ex-husband and thinks often of remarrying him though she recently refused to have intercourse with him. She seems to accept herself and to be quite self-assured.

Session 25.—She dreamed during the week she was having intercourse with a man. There was nothing else of importance. Interpretation: This is a "normal" dream for a young person. She now seems fully separated from the mother-therapist.

Addendum

In spite of the apparent completion of her separation she telephoned in a few weeks for another session.

Session 26.—Things have been going badly; she dislikes her job, has had difficulty with her child and her older brother, and complains of everything. She dreamed she was getting married to a woman; the therapist was there; things did not seem right and she asked him what to do; he said she would have to use her finger; she finally decided she would have to marry her ex-husband. Interpretation: She presents two alternatives: one, a return to her narcissism (attachment to the therapist), the other, marriage to her ex-husband. She was told almost nothing in the hope that she herself would be able to make her own choice. But it is evident to the therapist that this strongly sexed young woman must now find a suitable man onto whom she can attach her libido.

Session 27.—She complained of speech difficulties, of hating her job, and of wanting to quit it. She is completely dispirited. She was not encouraged but was told that she was wavering between returning to her old self or going ahead with her development, that she had already shown she was capable of making her own choice, and that no one could help her unless she was willing to help herself.

Session 28.—She seems much better and says she and her ex-husband have discussed remarriage; she has had normal, satisfactory sexual intercourse with him but decided not to do it again unless they do remarry. She realizes she has to keep "on the job" and to keep trying every minute of the time if she is to "make the grade."

These postfinale sessions show first how strong was her tendency to destroy herself by clinging to the mother-therapist, and second that he must take a firm attitude under these circumstances. Her pitiful, dispirited appeal was a mere act put on to fool both herself and him; for him it would have been naïve to take it at its face value, for her it might have been the *coup de grâce.*

And this situation emphasizes a point often made by Rank: psychotherapy is intended to show the patient she can make a choice; after this no one can make her take the right one; but if the therapist is bemused by the negativistic magic of her words and himself attempts to make her take it, then all may be undone.

Discussion of Second Treated Case

The details of the family life during this patient's infancy are not available as she dismissed the mother without further ado as insane and the father as a "bum." One may infer that the home was broken up shortly after the arrival of the younger brother and that the attitude toward the father came with later realization that he had no love for his children.

But the object hunger which was unsatisfied in the patient's previous married life appeared at once with projection of her superego and of her biological self onto the mother-therapist. The emission of urine instead of semen during intercourse in Session 2, Dream 2, would point to a boy, not a man, as the person with whom she identified, and we may surmise that this was the younger brother. This would establish the relationship with him as the secondary cause of the neurosis. And her reaction to this male identification is shown clearly in Session 3, Dream 2, where she is furious because she has not been given a dress indicating femininity.

Her projection of this identification onto the therapist seems to have given her some relief from it for in the very next session (4) she comes into libidinous relation with him: she still plays the adolescent masculine role but now has the mother all to herself; the brother is out of the way. And this points out the method by which she will also shed her infantile attachment to the mother-therapist, by which in fact, the effects of all negative identifications are shed in the psychotherapeutic situation: they are projected onto the passive therapist and left behind on departure from him.

Progress is rapid after this: in Session 6 she is already projecting her libido onto a young man, and in Sessions 7, 8, and 9 she is developing independence of the mother-therapist. But this independence is to a great extent a sadistic denial of the infantile attachment to the mother, as later events show.

After the final date is set the strength of her denial is revealed by the fact that three sessions (10, 11, and 12) pass before its full impact on feeling and libido is realized: not until Session 13 does this occur; and not until Session 14 does she have the dream of miraculous rebirth, and visualize the phallus in association with libido, i.e., overcome her denial of the male genitalia. This rebirth is followed by separation from the mother (Session 15, Dream 1) and the destruction of her world by fire and flood (Session 15, Dream 2); and this in turn by the symbolic portrayal of the death of the therapist (Session 16, Dream 2) and the revival of her libido (Session 16, Dream 3).

Here, then, the ego portrays the phases of its own psychological maturation in the same creative, allegorical symbolism that we find in early Egyptian, Sumerian, Judaic, and Christian cultures: death and regeneration in the travail of rebirth.

It is particularly interesting that during her period of recovery from this travail she contrasts her biological self and her mature, more adjusted self (Session 20, Dream 1) by indicating that the mature self can now accept and use as decoration the effect of culture (the psychotherapy) on nature, but that the biological self still protests to some extent.

In Session 21, Dream 1, one sees again the tendency to revert to the past by chance association with someone out of this past, in this case her ex-husband, but she reasserts her sexual maturation in the last two sessions, 24 and 25. Even then the actual termination of the psychotherapy brings on a temporary wavering in her ability to maintain her more mature self.

There can be little question that reversion to her former self and all her pain and suffering stem primarily from the attachment of the libido to the original mother object; this attachment is associated with such strong feelings that they are at first denied and even when admitted are overcome with great pain. Her denial of the maternal bond was later complicated by denial of the genitalia of the younger brother. But when she put him aside by projecting him onto the therapist there still remained the primary infantile libidinous attachment to the mother which she also projected onto the therapist and left behind on her final departure.

EPILOGUE

The unexpected anatomic and physiologic support for Rank's conception of an ego structure emphasizes the depth of his understanding of the human being. This develops from familiarity with the psychotherapeutic situation, where the psychic mechanisms are seen in operation, for it is these which really show how the psyche functions. The most natural of these, projection, may be used in either a negative or a positive sense; negatively by the opposing will as a means of shifting responsibility onto an outside source, and positively by the conscious will as a means of establishing a feeling relationship with another person. In this latter sense it is the source of all man's satisfactions from the transitional stage of sexual love to the maturity of creative achievement. Its counterpart, identification, is the means by which the opposing will adopts an attitude toward the world about it and so plays an important part in the formation of character. Since the opposing will controls the development of the primitive will to some extent its identification with the milieu may influence both will forces favorably or unfavorably. The denial mechanism operates between these two in such a way as to moderate the effects of one on the other. While just as vital as the other two for normal function of the psyche this mechanism has the greatest troublemaking potentialities because it may permit the ethical influence of the superego to be denied.

The operation of these mechanisms has been illustrated in a practical way by the synopsis of two treated cases where the tendency of the will forces to create *unreal* allegorical situations has been demonstrated. But the will forces themselves are plainly discernible behind the situations they project onto the screen of consciousness. The value of the psychotherapeutic relationship lies in the fact that it reveals to the patient certain facts he has hitherto denied. But since the average person may successfully deny the same facts it is not so much the denial that disturbs the neurotic as awareness of his own self-deception. In other words, it is primarily his self-awareness which makes him different from other men.

Self-awareness is increasingly apparent in modern man and the neurotic personality is merely an extreme example of its development. It makes him look with disbelief on the authorities to whom he has previously turned for guidance about right and wrong, makes him irreligious, but at the same time leaves him unconvinced that the power to make the decisions lies within himself. It is this that leads to *self-realization* and he can no more turn back from it than he can from progress in the physical sciences. Indeed, the present work seems to show that moral decisions derive from a structural character established in the prefrontal lobe at an early age as the product of interaction of opposing will, primitive will, and milieu and that in this sense they are as much the result of physical forces as motion in an automobile. The bright sunlight of self-realization dispels the mist of magic that for so long has covered the operation of these will forces; it takes the responsibility for one's aims and self-restraint out of a world of unreality and places it squarely on the shoulders of the individual.

The word "spiritual" is commonly used in a sense which gives it an unreal priestly sanctity and naïvely applies it to all matters connected with the projection of the superego onto a supernatural being. In this book it is used to describe a part of the ego whose demands are above and beyond those of the milieu. The average man is often irreligious, but projection of his superego is still as necessary to him as the air he breathes; now he makes public opinion his superego (and the love object his ideal) and so becomes more behavioristic and less spiritual. But this leaves him without convictions of his own and consequently makes him subject to the stronger wills of other persons and receptive to propaganda that appeals to his self-interest.

This lack of convictions and this receptivity for propaganda from others are of the greatest significance in the present cataclysmic struggle of Western man against the barbaric titans from the East. For this struggle illustrates on an international scale the same old battle that has so long been waged between the opposing will and feeling. On the Eastern side are cold, ruthless leaders who deny a feeling relationship to their own peoples, seize power over them, deprive them of all means of self-determination or self-defense, maintain their own eminence by the cruelest of tyrannies, and justify themselves by the self-righteous pretense that it will some day lead to the millenium of a classless society. Their indirect approach to victory over the West is by a sly, subversive appeal to the cupidity of the unfortunate and maladjusted, their direct approach by the threat of overwhelming force. Here is an obvious manifestation of the negativistic opposing will, which of necessity is accompanied by guilt and fear; but they deny the guilt and justify the fear by imputing (projecting) their own evil will to the West. The full significance of their malevolent denial of feeling can be realized by recalling that after seizing power they at first attempted to destroy the previous social structure formed on the basis of family life and religious belief: divorce was granted on mere appeal to their authority; children thus deprived of parents were indoctrinated by the state; the prevailing religious system was derided and suppressed, its previous deity symbolically supplanted by the embalmed corpse of the first of these leaders. And now that this power has been firmly established they attempt to maintain the fealty of the enslaved masses by a system of rewards and punishments equally as formal as the religion that preceded it: they present the portrait of the omnipotent leader to view for worship at every turn; it is to him that thanks are due for the material benefits of collectivism; it is he who makes the secret police a superego for the masses, who makes liquidation or a slave labor camp the penalty for deviation. In short, they now reproduce on a completely materialistic plane the system so ruthlessly expunged from the spiritual plane. The difference between the two systems lies in their ethical values. In the religious system the superego was projected onto an ethical deity; his was the power to judge between right and wrong; man was to blame for sin and disaster. In the present materialistic system expediency alone determines action; but this heroic acceptance for the responsibility of decisions by leaders without ethical values invites disaster. The flaw in their system stems from a primitive acceptance of the sadistic opposing will, from denial of their superego, and projection of the resulting fear onto the West. The iron curtain thus becomes a materialistic representative of the denial mechanism: on the one hand it is an attempt to prevent a feeling relationship between the East and West; on the other it is a guilty attempt to hide the consequences of their own evil actions.

The whole episode is parallel to that of a cold-blooded man of action who denies his own superego and finds a convenient ideology to justify the expression of his sadistic will forces; he feels no pangs of guilt because he projects his superego onto the very public authorities who later apprehend him and whom he egotistically believes he can outwit; he feels no remorse until he *is* apprehended and then not because of his own action but only because he was not smart enough to evade his pursuers. This creatively negativistic man of action rationalizes himself but almost inevitably meets his nemesis, for human beings have always instinctively protected themselves against him by taking over the punishing authority of the superego he so naïvely projects onto them.

On the Western side the danger is not of leaders with too much sadistic will but of those softened by too much feeling. For the psychotherapeutic situation shows that an excess of maternal feeling permits the child to retain an infantile attachment to support on the one hand and to suppress resentment against it on the other. This results first in psychological immaturity, later in improvidence, unfitness, and in the belief that rewards are due without individual effort, eventually in weaking of the will to resist aggression. And treatment of the neurotic shows that many who have succumbed to the pressure of outside aggression can only be helped by putting them in a situation of their own making where they must struggle to survive. The battle of the will forces against the superego in the individual thus finds an international parallel.

The significance of this conflict between the dynamic will forces and the restraint imposed on them by the ethical superego can scarcely be fully appreciated without some consideration of the religions which reveal man's spiritual development in historical perspective. When these religions are studied with the principles of the will psychology and their anatomical substrata in mind it is possible to see that religious systems are projections which represent different portions of the central nervous system. The moral values which originate in these structures are almost a question of life or death for the present-day neurotic who projects his superego, from which they derive, onto the therapist and so makes him responsible for them. They were equally important in earlier times but man was much more naïve then, took his dreams at their face value, and projected the responsibility for decisions about right or wrong onto a deity. When these religions are studied further with the various stages of psychological immaturity in mind it is possible to see that the vigor and ability of a people to maintain itself run roughly parallel with its religious system.

Thus when man had to struggle for a bare existence in a hard and unrelenting world of enemies the sadistic opposing will by which he maintained himself was projected onto an evil deity, the prince of darkness, and the reaction of the superego against it onto a stern, punishing god. As he became less nomadic and warlike, developed an agricultural economy and a fixed abode, his god changed to one who created the earth, the sea, and all living creatures, who made man in his own image. This creative god that we find in the Bible was both a justification and a denial of the ancient Jews' creative will because they imputed it to their deity.

The same forces that appeared in the dream and in Judaism we see at work in the Greek civilization but with this difference: instead of projecting onto a single punishing deity the Greeks accepted much of the responsibility for the human passions and frailties and justified them more or less frivolously by projecting them onto separate deities. This dispersion of the conscious will meant the acceptance of what we have seen earlier in this work to be states of psychological immaturity, and the overwhelming guilt that arose from it was clearly portrayed by the tragic fates of Prometheus and Oedipus. It resulted in a high degree of sophistication and civilization but in a moral disintegration which culminated in the Roman patriarchy. The final fall of this state before the barbarian onslaught may be attributed to the same cynical acceptance of the dispersion of the conscious will and the ensuing consciousness of guilt. We find then that when fear of the superego is maintained in a monotheistic religion vigor is maintained but civilization is less sophisticated; per contra, when the superego is disregarded and all human developmental frailties are accepted and justified by a pantheistic religion there results a high degree of sophistication and civilization accompanied by consciousness of guilt, moral disintegration, and failure to maintain the State.

Christianity undoubtedly arose as a reaction to the degeneracy of the Roman patriarchy and combined the Jews' monotheism with a new consideration for the *individual* which it symbolized by the Son. This asexual figure, half man, half god, triumphed not by force of will but meekly, by force of spirit. Here finally was acceptance of the conscious individual will as opposed to the cruel opposing will and the punishing superego of early Judaism. Here was acceptance of the conscious individual will cleansed of the licentiousness of unrestrained libido and accompanied by a maternal protective figure, revered for her purity. Christianity integrated what had gone before and thus represents an overcoming of the sadistic opposing will and the stern punishing superego, a timid acceptance of the conscious individual will under protection of a maternal figure and submission to the superego through love instead of through fear.

The whole historical sequence of religious development in man deals with the identical forces discussed in the will psychology and seen operating in the psychotherapeutic experience of the self-conscious neurotic. But in this experience both the cruel opposing will and the superego must be accepted as forces within the self whereas in early times they had to be projected onto supernatural beings.

In the Prologue of this book the present writer has indicated that identification of the will forces and the superego in himself as well as in his patients has contributed to his understanding of Rank's ego structure and to its depiction in diagrammatic form. This led inevitably to his consideration of man's conscience, represented here by the superego, as a governing force in the psyche, and, finally, as the absolute authority in the sense of Kant's categorical imperative. He then discovered three things: first, that both the will forces and the superego found what seemed to be anatomic representation in the brain structure; second, that the opposing will could indeed gradually be consciously controlled so as to bring it under the influence of the superego; and third, that this control modified the form of expression of the conscious will. And so, at long last, he came to a full realization of the significance of Rank's will psychology and of the greatness of its contribution to the resolution of man's ethical problem.[1] This realization makes obligatory the process of integration described in this book and terminates in the true assessment of the capabilities of the individual and their full application to the problems of life with his fellow man. This is not to say, however, that such integration must be set up as an ideal for every patient. The degree

---

[1] Rank's work developed from collaboration with the group of associates that gathered about Freud to whom credit for his ideas is therefore partly due. For the three levels designated as the id, the ego, and the superego are not original with Rank. But since in his earliest works he emphasized the element of restraint that lay within the ego, the concept of the social self, the development of a genetic psychology, and so, eventually, of the ego structure, must be attributed to him. Surely history will place this man among the greatest creative thinkers.

to which each of them becomes integrated will depend on individual factors, but the conflict of diverging tendencies brought on by increasing self-awareness in the neurotic type makes the peace of mind and intellectual clarification which follow this integration more and more necessary for him.

Western man is presently in a self-conscious, transitional stage where to many the moral restraints that derive from religious projection of the will and superego onto a supreme being no longer seem real. This state of transition often results in much loss of restraint, in rationalization of the will to do as one pleases, in the attempt to overcome and deny the fear inevitably connected with this rationalization, and eventually in more or less self-destruction and moral disintegration. The reversal of this process can occur most easily in youth and then only by individual assumption of the restraint originally projected away and now so commonly disregarded altogether. It may be aided by an understanding of the ego structure and its possible anatomic substrata. Since the fate of the younger generation lies in the hands of our educators, sociologists, and scientists, it is to them that this book is particularly addressed in the hope that it will give them greater understanding of the developmental processes that precede real maturity. For the significance of this understanding transcends the treatment of the neurotic.

INDEX

orgasm, 65, 73, 77; orgiastic epileptiform attack, 74

Papez, James W., 57 n., 73 n., 98
paracentral lobule, 73, 74, 75, 77
paranoia, 30
parasympathetic, 64, 67, 77
pars magnocellularis, 62, 65, 67, 77, 78; parvicellularis, 59, 72
Penfield, Wilder, 73 n., 103, 111
perceptual faculties, 105
periamygdaloid cortex, 77
perineal sphincters, 74
periventricular system, 67, 77
personality, 53, 54, 102; creative, 6; expression of, 54, 55
phobias, 26, 27
pituitary, 64, 81
pneumotaxic center, 70
postural reflexes, 89
pre-Christian era, 143–44
preoptic area, 77
prepyriform area, 77, 101, 107
projections, 11, 35, 37, 42, 43, 46, 140; extrapyramidal, 53; of maternal restraints, 26; negative, 8, 11, 18, 33; positive, 8, 11, 18, 29; pyramidal, 53
Prometheus, 143
psychical seizures, 108, 109
psychological aberration, 57
psychoses, 29, 34
psychosomatic disease, 26, 65
psychotherapeutic situation, 7–11, 17, 33, 36, 39, 42–46, 140–45; analyses of case histories in, 124–27, 138–39; synopses of case histories in, 113–24, 127–38
pulvinar, 49
putamen, 89

rage, sham, 65
Rank, Otto, 1, 2, 3, 7, 16, 17, 32, 33, 47, 97, 98, 104, 140, 144
Ransom, S. W., 3
Rasmussen, Th., 73 n.
rationalization of will, 81
respiratory center, 69, 70
reticular formation, 89
rhinencephalon, 72

sadismus, oral, 17, 18, 21, 23, 33
sado-masochistic mechanism, 30, 44, 63
schizophrenia, 59
self: biological, 5, 10, 33, 34, 36, 82, 101; social, 6, 34, 36, 82, 144; spiritual, 7, 36

sex differences, 14, 15, 25
sexual impulses, 101
sexual intercourse, 73, 75
sexual object, 20, 21; shift of, 21
sibling, advent of, 14–15, 24
sleep function, 71
speech, 78; origin of, 91
sphincter ego, 74
spinocerebellar tracts, 94, 95
stammering, 60
stratum zonale, 49
stria medullaris, 77
substantia nigra, 89
superego, 2, 22, 35, 36, 38, 39, 57, 62, 64, 74, 101, 141–45; beginning of, 19; development of, 14; doubling of from advent of sibling, 15; subsidiary, 106, 108
suppression, 83, 86
suppressor bands, 76, 85, 89, 99
sympathetic activity, 67

Taft, Jessie, 2 n.
tangential fibers, 78
tegmentum, 67
temper tantrums, 86
temporal lobe, 78; tip of, 99, 102
temporal neocortex, 110
thalamus, 47; anterior pole of, 49; geniculate bodies, 56; internal medullary lamina of, 49; posterior group of nuclei, 49; pulvinar, 49, 58; stratum zonale of, 49; ventral group of nuclei, 49
toilet training, 14, 19, 24
transference, 7; see also psychotherapeutic situation
trauma of birth, 72
Tromner, E., 71 n.
Turner, R. S., 4

unconscious, 35, 36

vagina, 73; dentata, 81
vestibular nuclei, 94

Wall, Patrick, 64
Ward and McColloch, 68
weaning time, 14, 28
Wilbur, Ray Lyman, 2 n.
will, 33, 37, 38, 43–46, 72, 140–45; conscious (will), 35–39, 43, 76; content of, 34; expression of, 82; opposing (will), 33, 35–39, 43, 59, 62, 68, 72, 74; primitive (will), 43, 68, 74, 141; rationalization of, 35; reinforcement of, 91